Carnivore Diet Energy Boost Cookbook

A 90-Day Science-Based Food Protocol with Quick & Easy Recipes to Eliminate Brain Fog and Chronic Fatigue Permanently

THOMAS CURTNEY

Thomas Curtney © Copyright 2024. All rights reserved.

The content contained within this book may not be reproduced, duplicated, or transmitted without direct written permission from the author or the publisher.

Under no circumstances will any blame or legal responsibility be held against the publisher, or author, for any damages, reparation, or monetary loss due to the information contained within this book, either directly or indirectly.

Legal Notice:

This book is copyright-protected. It is only for personal use. You cannot amend, distribute, sell, use, quote or paraphrase any part, or the content within this book, without the consent of the author or publisher.

Disclaimer Notice:

Please note the information contained within this document is for educational and entertainment purposes only. All effort has been executed to present accurate, up-to-date, reliable, and complete information. No warranties of any kind are declared or implied. Readers acknowledge that the author is not engaging in the rendering of legal, financial, medical or professional advice. The content within this book has been derived from various sources. Please consult a licensed professional before attempting any techniques outlined in this book.

By reading this document, the reader agrees that under no circumstances is the author responsible for any losses, direct or indirect, that are incurred as a result of the use of the information contained within this document, including, but not limited to, errors, omissions, or inaccuracies.

TABLE OF CONTENTS

PART 1: INTRODUCTION TO THE CARNIVORE DIET 5

CHAPTER 1: UNDERSTANDING THE CARNIVORE DIET 5
- What is the Carnivore Diet? 5
- Common Myths and Misconceptions 5

Chapter 2: Benefits of the Carnivore Diet 8
- Enhanced Energy Levels: How the Diet Fuels Your Body 8
- Mental Clarity and Focus: Eliminating Brain Fog 9
- Weight Loss and Body Composition 10
- Improved Digestion and Gut Health 11

Chapter 3: The 90-Day Scientific Food Protocol 13
- Overview of the 90-Day Plan 13
- Setting Your Goals: What to Expect in 90 Days 14
- 90-Days Complete Meal Plan 16

PART 2: CARNIVORE DIET RECIPES BY FOOD CATEGORY 21

Chapter 6: Meat Recipes 22
Beef Recipes 22
- Beef and Bacon Skewers Recipe 22
- Beef Bone Marrow and Steak Recipe 22
- Beef Liver and Onion Recipe 23
- Beef Meatballs Recipe 23
- Beef Short Ribs Recipe 24
- Ground Beef and Egg Scramble Recipe 24
- New York Strip Steak with Herb Butter Recipe 25
- Pepper-Crusted Steak Recipe 25
- Seared Beef Tips Recipe 26
- Slow-Cooked Brisket Recipe 26

Pork Recipes 27
- Bacon-Wrapped Pork Chops Recipe 27
- Carnivore Pork Belly Bites Recipe 27
- Crispy Pork Rinds Recipe 28
- Garlic Butter Pork Tenderloin Recipe 28
- Grilled Pork Loin Recipe 29
- Pan-Seared Pork Medallions Recipe 29
- Pork and Egg Breakfast Skillet Recipe 30
- Pork Shoulder Roast Recipe 30
- Pulled Pork Recipe 31
- Simple Pork Sausage Patties Recipe 31

Lamb Recipes 32
- Braised Lamb Shanks Recipe 32
- Grilled Lamb T-Bone Recipe 32
- Garlic Butter Lamb Chops Recipe 33
- Grilled Lamb Skewers Recipe 33
- Homemade Lamb Sausages Recipe 34
- Lamb and Egg Scramble 34
- Lamb Meatballs Recipe 35
- Lamb with Thyme and Lemon Recipe 35
- Minted Lamb Stew Recipe 36
- Roasted Lamb with Rosemary Recipe 36

Chapter 7: Poultry Recipes 37
Chicken Recipes 37
- Bacon-Wrapped Chicken Breasts Recipe 37
- Baked Chicken Drumsticks Recipe 37
- Chicken and Bacon Skewers Recipe 38
- Chicken Breast with Lemon Butter Recipe 38
- Crispy Chicken Wings Recipe 39
- Grilled Chicken Drumsticks Recipe 39
- Herbed Chicken Wings Recipe 40
- Pan-Fried Chicken Breasts Recipe 40
- Roasted Chicken Quarters Recipe 41
- Spicy Chicken Wings Recipe 41

Turkey Recipes 42
- Butter-Basted Turkey Thighs Recipe 42
- Grilled Turkey Burgers Recipe 42
- Herbed Turkey Cutlets Recipe 43
- Pan-Fried Turkey Sausage Patties Recipe 43
- Roasted Turkey Tenderloins Recipe 44
- Slow-Cooked Turkey Breast Recipe 44
- Spicy Turkey Meatballs Recipe 45
- Turkey Breast with Lemon Butter Recipe 45
- Turkey Thighs with Sage Butter Recipe 46
- Smoked Turkey Thighs Recipe 46

Duck Recipes 47
- Cajun-Spiced Duck Breast Recipe 47
- Crispy Duck Skin Chips Recipe 47
- Duck Breast with Black Pepper Butter Recipe 48
- Duck Breast with Rosemary Butter Recipe 48
- Duck Confit with Garlic and Thyme Recipe 49
- Duck Fat Roasted Whole Duck with Thyme Recipe 49
- Duck Thighs with Garlic Butter and Thyme Recipe 50
- Garlic Herb Duck Wings Recipe 50
- Roasted Duck Breast with Sage Recipe 51
- Spicy Duck Drumsticks with Sage Recipe 51

CHAPTER 8: FISH AND SEAFOOD RECIPES 52
Fish Recipes 52
- Baked Cod with Lemon Butter Recipe 52

Baked Salmon with Dill Recipe	52
Roasted Sea Bass Recipe	53
Sardines in Olive Oil Recipe	53
Thyme-Basted Trout Recipe	54
Seafood Recipes	**55**
Butter-Basted Lobster Tails Recipe	55
Cajun-Spiced Shrimp Recipe	55
Grilled Shrimp Skewers Recipe	56
Sauteed Shrimp with Butter Recipe	56
Spicy Garlic Shrimp Recipe	57
Shellfish Recipes	**58**
Bacon-Wrapped Scallops Recipe	58
Grilled Oysters Recipe	58
Lemon Butter Scallops Recipe	59
Pan-Fried Clams Recipe	59
Seafood Medley in Garlic Butter Recipe	60
CHAPTER 9: EGG RECIPES	**61**
Breakfast Recipes	**61**
Bacon and Egg Scramble Recipe	61
Egg and Sausage Breakfast Skillet Recipe	61
Eggs Benedict Carnivore Style Recipe	62
Omelette with Bacon and Cheese Recipe	62
Steak and Egg Breakfast Bowl Recipe	63
Lunch and Dinner Recipes	**64**
Beef and Egg Stir-Fry Recipe	64
Cheesy Egg-Stuffed Meatballs Recipe	64
Chicken and Egg Drop Soup Recipe	65
Salmon and Egg Casserole Recipe	65
Turkey and Egg Bake Recipe	66
Snacks and Sides	**67**
Creamy Egg Salad Recipe	67
Egg and Sausage Muffin Cups Recipe	67
Mini Egg Frittatas Recipe	68
Soft-Boiled Eggs with Herb Butter Recipe	68
Spicy Deviled Eggs Recipe	69
PART 3: SUPPORTING YOUR CARNIVORE JOURNEY	**70**
Chapter 10: Supplementing on the Carnivore Diet	**70**
Do You Need Supplements? The Debate	70
Finding the Right Balance	71
Recommended Supplements for Carnivore Dieters	73
Chapter 11: Hydration and Electrolyte Balance	**76**
The Importance of Hydration on the Carnivore Diet	76
Best Practices for Staying Hydrated	77
Conclusion	**80**
APPENDICES	**81**
Grocery Lists for Each Week	**81**

PART 1: INTRODUCTION TO THE CARNIVORE DIET

Welcome to the world of the Carnivore Diet, a unique approach to nutrition that focuses on consuming only animal-based foods. This diet challenges conventional wisdom by eliminating all plant-based foods, emphasizing the simplicity and nutrient density found in meat, fish, eggs, and dairy. Whether you're here to improve your health, boost energy, or explore new dietary territory, this book will guide you through the science, benefits, and practicalities of the Carnivore Diet. Let's embark on this journey together, discovering how a meat-focused diet can transform your well-being and reshape your relationship with food.

CHAPTER 1: UNDERSTANDING THE CARNIVORE DIET

WHAT IS THE CARNIVORE DIET?

The Carnivore Diet is a way of eating that is as straightforward as it is revolutionary: it involves consuming only animal-based foods. At its core, this diet includes meat, fish, eggs, and certain dairy products, while completely eliminating all plant-based foods. The idea behind the Carnivore Diet is rooted in the belief that humans thrive on a diet that mirrors what our ancestors consumed for thousands of years before the advent of agriculture and processed foods.

You might be wondering, "Why exclude plant foods entirely?" The answer lies in both the nutritional composition of animal products and the potential issues that some people experience with plant-based foods. Animal products are incredibly nutrient-dense, providing all the essential amino acids, vitamins, and minerals your body needs, often in more bioavailable forms than those found in plants. This means your body can absorb and utilize these nutrients more efficiently.

Moreover, some individuals find that plant foods can contribute to digestive discomfort, inflammation, or autoimmune reactions. By removing these potential irritants, the Carnivore Diet aims to simplify your nutrition and allow your body to function optimally. You're essentially giving your digestive system a break from dealing with the fibers, antinutrients, and complex carbohydrates present in plants, which can sometimes be challenging for the body to process.

Another key aspect of the Carnivore Diet is its focus on fat and protein as primary energy sources. By cutting out carbohydrates, your body shifts into a state of ketosis, where it burns fat for fuel instead of glucose. This metabolic shift can lead to a range of benefits, from sustained energy levels and mental clarity to improved metabolic health.

The Carnivore Diet isn't just about eating more meat; it's about adopting a nutritional approach that simplifies your diet, reduces potential triggers for inflammation, and focuses on foods that are rich in essential nutrients. Whether you're seeking weight loss, better digestion, or a general improvement in well-being, the Carnivore Diet offers a unique path to achieving these goals by returning to the basics of human nutrition.

COMMON MYTHS AND MISCONCEPTIONS

When it comes to the Carnivore Diet, there are numerous myths and misconceptions that can create confusion and skepticism. As with any diet that challenges mainstream nutritional advice, it's important to separate fact from fiction to make informed decisions about your health. Let's address some of the most common myths and misconceptions surrounding the Carnivore Diet and clarify what the science and real-world experience actually tell us.

Myth 1: The Carnivore Diet Is Nutritionally Deficient

One of the most pervasive myths is that the Carnivore Diet lacks essential nutrients because it excludes all plant-based foods. Many people believe that without fruits, vegetables, and grains, you'll miss out on vital vitamins, minerals, and fiber. However, this misconception overlooks the nutrient density of animal products. Animal-based foods provide nearly all the essential nutrients your body needs, often in more bioavailable forms than plant foods. For instance, vitamin B12, which is crucial for nerve function and energy production, is found exclusively in animal products. Additionally, nutrients like heme iron, zinc, and vitamin K2 are more readily absorbed and utilized by the body when sourced from animal foods. While it's true that the Carnivore Diet doesn't provide dietary fiber, many people find that they don't need fiber for digestive health once they remove the foods that cause gastrointestinal distress.

Myth 2: Eating Meat Is Bad for Your Heart

Another common concern is that consuming large amounts of meat, especially red meat, will increase the risk of heart disease due to its saturated fat content. This belief stems from outdated dietary guidelines that linked saturated fat to elevated cholesterol levels and heart disease. However, recent research has debunked this association. Studies have shown that there is no clear link between saturated fat intake and heart disease. In fact, some evidence suggests that a diet rich in animal fats can improve heart health by raising HDL (the "good" cholesterol) and improving triglyceride levels. The Carnivore Diet's emphasis on whole, unprocessed meats also means you're avoiding the harmful trans fats and refined sugars that are actually associated with heart disease.

Myth 3: The Carnivore Diet Will Lead to Kidney Damage

There's a widespread belief that a high-protein diet, such as the Carnivore Diet, can cause kidney damage, particularly in people with pre-existing kidney conditions. However, this is largely a myth. For healthy individuals, there is no scientific evidence to support the idea that consuming large amounts of protein will harm the kidneys. The myth likely originated from the fact that people with chronic kidney disease (CKD) are often advised to limit protein intake to reduce the workload on their kidneys. But for those with normal kidney function, the body is fully capable of processing higher levels of protein without any adverse effects. In fact, protein plays a vital role in maintaining muscle mass, supporting immune function, and regulating various metabolic processes.

Myth 4: The Carnivore Diet Causes Nutrient Deficiencies Over Time

Another misconception is that while the Carnivore Diet may work in the short term, it will eventually lead to nutrient deficiencies if followed long-term. Critics argue that the lack of plant-based foods could result in deficiencies in vitamins like C and E, or minerals like magnesium. However, those who follow the Carnivore Diet often find that their nutrient levels remain stable or even improve over time. For instance, while vitamin C is commonly associated with fruits and vegetables, small amounts are present in raw organ meats and even muscle meats. Additionally, the reduced need for antioxidants like vitamin C may be linked to the lower levels of oxidative stress and inflammation on a Carnivore Diet, as the diet eliminates many inflammatory foods.

Myth 5: The Carnivore Diet Is Unsustainable

A common argument against the Carnivore Diet is that it's unsustainable in the long term due to its restrictive nature. Critics claim that it's difficult to stick to such a limited range of foods and that the diet lacks variety, which can lead to boredom and diet fatigue. However, sustainability is highly individual. Many people find the simplicity of the Carnivore Diet to be one of its strengths, as it removes the complexity of meal planning and decision-making. Additionally, the satiety provided by high-protein, high-fat meals can make it easier to adhere to the diet without experiencing hunger or cravings. For those who enjoy the foods allowed on the Carnivore Diet, it can be a sustainable and enjoyable way of eating.

Myth 6: The Carnivore Diet Is Harmful to Gut Health

Some people worry that eliminating fiber from the diet, which is abundant in plant-based foods, will negatively affect gut health. Fiber is often touted as essential for healthy digestion and maintaining a diverse gut microbiome. However, the relationship between fiber and gut health is more complex than commonly believed. Many individuals on the Carnivore Diet report significant improvements in their digestive health, including relief from conditions like irritable bowel syndrome (IBS) and inflammatory bowel disease (IBD). This suggests that for some people, removing fiber and potentially irritating plant foods from the diet can lead to a healthier, more balanced gut. The Carnivore Diet's focus on easily digestible, nutrient-dense foods allows the gut to heal and function optimally without the need for fiber.

Myth 7: The Carnivore Diet Is Environmentally Unsustainable

Concerns about the environmental impact of a meat-heavy diet are frequently raised. Critics argue that raising livestock for meat consumption is resource-intensive and contributes to greenhouse gas emissions. While it's true that industrial farming practices can have negative environmental impacts, it's important to consider alternative approaches, such as regenerative agriculture. Regenerative farming practices, which focus on soil health, biodiversity, and sustainable land management, can actually reduce carbon emissions and improve environmental outcomes. Additionally, the Carnivore Diet can be more environmentally sustainable when you choose to source your meat from local, pasture-raised, and ethically managed farms.

CHAPTER 2: BENEFITS OF THE CARNIVORE DIET

ENHANCED ENERGY LEVELS: HOW THE DIET FUELS YOUR BODY

One of the most compelling benefits of the Carnivore Diet that many people experience is a significant and sustained increase in energy levels. If you've ever struggled with the highs and lows of energy throughout the day—feeling sluggish after meals or hitting that mid-afternoon slump—you'll be pleased to know that the Carnivore Diet has the potential to stabilize and enhance your energy in a way that few other diets can.

The secret behind this energy boost lies in how your body metabolizes the macronutrients—proteins and fats—that form the foundation of the Carnivore Diet. Unlike diets high in carbohydrates, which cause your blood sugar to spike and crash, the Carnivore Diet provides a steady, slow-burning source of fuel that keeps your energy levels consistent throughout the day.

When you consume carbohydrates, your body converts them into glucose, which then spikes your blood sugar and provides a quick burst of energy. However, this energy is often short-lived, and as your blood sugar levels drop, you're left feeling tired, hungry, and in need of another quick fix. This rollercoaster effect not only drains your energy but also increases your reliance on frequent meals or snacks to keep your energy levels up.

In contrast, the Carnivore Diet shifts your body into a different metabolic state—one that relies on fats and proteins as the primary sources of energy. Without the constant influx of carbohydrates, your body begins to adapt by burning fat for fuel, a process known as ketosis. When your body enters ketosis, it produces molecules called ketones, which serve as a highly efficient and stable energy source. These ketones can be used by your brain, muscles, and other organs, providing a consistent supply of energy that doesn't lead to the same peaks and valleys associated with glucose.

One of the key benefits of ketones is that they are a more efficient fuel for your brain. While your brain can function on glucose, it actually thrives on ketones, which cross the blood-brain barrier more easily and provide a steady source of energy. Many people on the Carnivore Diet report enhanced mental clarity, improved focus, and a greater sense of alertness—attributes that can be directly linked to the brain's utilization of ketones. This means that instead of feeling foggy or fatigued after meals, you're likely to feel clear-headed and ready to tackle whatever the day throws at you.

In addition to the cognitive benefits, the Carnivore Diet's focus on protein also plays a crucial role in maintaining energy levels. Protein is not only essential for building and repairing tissues but also has a significant impact on your metabolism. The thermic effect of protein—the amount of energy your body uses to digest, absorb, and metabolize it—is higher than that of fats or carbohydrates. This means that when you consume a meal rich in protein, your body is working harder, burning more calories, and ultimately sustaining a higher level of energy.

Moreover, protein's role in muscle maintenance and growth cannot be overlooked. When your muscles are well-nourished and strong, your overall energy expenditure increases, and you're better equipped to handle physical activities throughout the day. Whether you're engaging in strenuous exercise or simply going about your daily tasks, the Carnivore Diet provides the necessary fuel to keep your muscles functioning optimally, contributing to a sense of vitality and endurance.

Another factor contributing to the enhanced energy levels on the Carnivore Diet is the reduction of inflammatory foods. Many plant-based foods, particularly those high in sugar, grains, and processed carbohydrates, can contribute to systemic inflammation. Inflammation is not just a risk factor for chronic diseases; it also saps your energy by forcing your body to divert resources to combat this internal stress. By eliminating these foods and focusing on anti-inflammatory, nutrient-dense animal products, you reduce the overall burden on your body, freeing up energy that was previously being used to fight inflammation.

Finally, it's important to recognize that the Carnivore Diet supports stable energy levels by eliminating the need for frequent eating. On a high-carbohydrate diet, you may find yourself needing to eat every few hours to maintain your energy. However, because the Carnivore Diet provides such a sustained release of energy from fats and proteins, you can go longer between meals without feeling hungry or fatigued. This not only simplifies your daily routine but also reduces the likelihood of overeating or relying on energy-dense, nutrient-poor snacks.

MENTAL CLARITY AND FOCUS: ELIMINATING BRAIN FOG

One of the most striking and immediate benefits that many people experience when adopting the Carnivore Diet is a significant improvement in mental clarity and focus. If you've ever felt bogged down by a foggy mind, struggling to concentrate, or constantly fighting off the fatigue that drags on your productivity, you'll likely find the Carnivore Diet to be a game-changer in this regard.

The concept of "brain fog" is something most of us are familiar with, even if we haven't always had the words to describe it. It's that frustrating state where your thoughts feel sluggish, you have trouble recalling information, and your mental sharpness just isn't what it should be. While brain fog can be caused by a variety of factors—including stress, lack of sleep, and hormonal imbalances—one of the primary culprits is diet, particularly the consumption of foods that lead to fluctuations in blood sugar and contribute to inflammation in the brain.

The Carnivore Diet addresses brain fog by cutting out these dietary triggers and providing your brain with the nutrients it needs to function at its best. One of the most significant changes that occurs when you switch to a Carnivore Diet is the stabilization of blood sugar levels. On a typical diet that includes carbohydrates, your blood sugar can fluctuate wildly throughout the day, leading to corresponding highs and lows in your energy and mental clarity. These fluctuations can leave you feeling sharp one moment and mentally drained the next, making it difficult to maintain focus over longer periods.

By eliminating carbohydrates, the Carnivore Diet helps to stabilize your blood sugar, which in turn supports steady mental energy. Instead of relying on glucose, which can cause spikes and crashes, your brain begins to utilize ketones—a more stable and efficient energy source derived from fat. Ketones have been shown to provide a more consistent and sustained source of fuel for the brain, which translates into improved mental clarity, better concentration, and enhanced cognitive performance.

Another important factor in eliminating brain fog is the reduction of inflammation, particularly neuroinflammation. Many common foods, especially those high in sugar, refined grains, and industrial seed oils, can contribute to inflammation in the body and brain. Chronic inflammation can impair cognitive function, making it harder to think clearly and stay focused. The Carnivore Diet, by focusing exclusively on anti-inflammatory animal products and eliminating pro-inflammatory foods, can help reduce this inflammation and support a healthier brain environment.

Moreover, the Carnivore Diet is rich in essential nutrients that directly benefit brain health. Animal-based foods are abundant in omega-3 fatty acids, particularly DHA (docosahexaenoic acid), which is crucial for maintaining the structure and function of your brain cells. DHA is a major component of the brain's gray matter and is essential for cognitive function, memory, and overall mental well-being. By consuming foods like fatty fish and grass-fed meats, you're providing your brain with the building blocks it needs to operate at peak efficiency.

In addition to omega-3s, the Carnivore Diet is also rich in other brain-supporting nutrients like vitamin B12, iron, and choline. Vitamin B12, found exclusively in animal products, is vital for the production of neurotransmitters that regulate mood and cognition. A deficiency in B12 can lead to cognitive decline, memory problems, and increased brain fog. Iron is another critical nutrient that supports oxygen transport to the brain, ensuring that your brain cells have the oxygen they need to function properly. Choline, found in high amounts in eggs and liver, is essential for the production of acetylcholine, a neurotransmitter involved in learning and memory.

The cumulative effect of these nutrients, combined with the anti-inflammatory nature of the Carnivore Diet, creates an environment in which your brain can thrive. Many people on the Carnivore Diet report not only a reduction in brain fog but also an enhanced ability to focus for longer periods, quicker thinking, and improved problem-solving skills. This mental clarity is not just about feeling more alert; it's about being able to engage more fully in your work, hobbies, and relationships, free from the mental fatigue that once held you back.

It's also worth noting that the Carnivore Diet can have a stabilizing effect on mood, which further contributes to improved focus and mental clarity. Mood swings and mental fog often go hand in hand, with fluctuations in blood sugar and inflammation contributing to both. By leveling out these fluctuations and providing your brain with steady, nutrient-dense fuel, the Carnivore Diet can help you achieve a more balanced and focused mental state.

WEIGHT LOSS AND BODY COMPOSITION

When it comes to weight loss and improving body composition, the Carnivore Diet offers a unique and highly effective approach. Unlike many conventional diets that focus on calorie counting, portion control, or limiting specific macronutrients, the Carnivore Diet simplifies the process by focusing solely on nutrient-dense animal products. This not only makes it easier to follow but also addresses the underlying mechanisms that drive weight loss and fat reduction.

The first key to understanding why the Carnivore Diet is so effective for weight loss lies in its impact on your metabolism. By eliminating carbohydrates, your body shifts from using glucose as its primary energy source to burning fat for fuel—a metabolic state known as ketosis. In ketosis, your body becomes highly efficient at breaking down stored fat into fatty acids and converting them into ketones, which are then used for energy. This process not only leads to a reduction in body fat but also helps preserve lean muscle mass, which is crucial for maintaining a healthy metabolism.

One of the most significant advantages of the Carnivore Diet for weight loss is its ability to regulate insulin levels. Insulin is a hormone that plays a critical role in fat storage. When you consume carbohydrates, your blood sugar levels rise, prompting your pancreas to release insulin. Insulin helps shuttle glucose into your cells for energy, but it also signals your body to store excess glucose as fat. By minimizing carbohydrate intake, the Carnivore Diet keeps insulin levels low, reducing the body's tendency to store fat and encouraging it to burn fat instead.

Additionally, the Carnivore Diet's high protein content is a major factor in its effectiveness for weight loss. Protein is the most satiating macronutrient, meaning it helps you feel full and satisfied for longer periods. This naturally reduces your overall calorie intake without the need for deliberate restriction. When you're consuming nutrient-dense animal foods like beef, pork, poultry, and fish, you're more likely to eat until you're genuinely satisfied, rather than overeating due to cravings or hunger. This reduction in caloric intake, combined with the body's increased reliance on fat for energy, creates an ideal environment for weight loss.

Moreover, protein plays a vital role in preserving and building lean muscle mass, which is essential for a healthy body composition. Muscle tissue is metabolically active, meaning it burns more calories at rest compared to fat tissue. By maintaining or even increasing your muscle mass through a high-protein diet, you can enhance your resting metabolic rate, making it easier to burn calories and lose fat over time. This is particularly important as you lose weight, as it helps prevent the common issue of losing muscle along with fat, which can slow down your metabolism and make further weight loss more difficult.

The Carnivore Diet also excels at reducing visceral fat, the harmful fat that surrounds your internal organs and is associated with an increased risk of chronic diseases like heart disease, diabetes, and metabolic syndrome. Visceral fat is particularly responsive to dietary changes that lower insulin and inflammation—two areas where the Carnivore Diet shines. By eliminating processed foods, sugars, and inflammatory oils, and replacing them with anti-inflammatory, nutrient-rich animal products, you create a hormonal environment that promotes the reduction of visceral fat and improves overall health.

Another important aspect of the Carnivore Diet's impact on body composition is its role in reducing inflammation. Chronic inflammation is a significant contributor to obesity and metabolic dysfunction. Foods high in sugar, refined carbohydrates, and industrial seed oils can trigger inflammatory responses in the body, leading to insulin resistance, increased fat storage, and difficulty losing weight. The Carnivore Diet eliminates these pro-inflammatory foods and focuses on whole, unprocessed meats and animal fats, which have anti-inflammatory properties. This reduction in inflammation can not only accelerate weight loss but also improve overall metabolic health, making it easier to achieve and maintain a leaner body composition.

It's also worth noting that the Carnivore Diet can help regulate appetite and cravings in a way that many other diets cannot. Carbohydrates, especially refined carbs and sugars can trigger cravings and lead to overeating. These foods cause rapid spikes and crashes in blood sugar, which can create a cycle of hunger and overeating. On the Carnivore Diet, the absence of these blood sugar fluctuations leads to more stable energy levels and a reduction in cravings. Many people find that they can go longer between meals and are less likely to snack or overeat, which further supports weight loss and a healthier body composition.

Finally, the Carnivore Diet's simplicity is one of its greatest strengths when it comes to weight loss. There's no need to count calories, track macros, or adhere to complicated meal plans. Instead, you focus on eating nutrient-dense animal foods until you're satisfied. This simplicity makes it easier to stay consistent, which is key to long-term success. The diet naturally leads to a reduction in overall calorie intake, increased fat burning, and improved body composition without the need for restrictive dieting or constant monitoring.

IMPROVED DIGESTION AND GUT HEALTH

One of the most surprising benefits that many people experience on the Carnivore Diet is a dramatic improvement in digestion and gut health. If you've struggled with digestive issues such as bloating, gas, constipation, or irritable bowel syndrome (IBS), you may find that the Carnivore Diet offers a level of relief that other diets have not. Understanding how and why this diet can be so effective for gut health requires a closer look at the relationship between the foods you eat and the health of your digestive system.

At the core of the Carnivore Diet's impact on digestion is its simplicity. By focusing exclusively on animal-based foods, you're eliminating many of the common dietary triggers that can cause digestive distress. Foods like grains, legumes, and certain vegetables contain compounds such as lectins, phytates, and oxalates, which can be difficult for some people to digest. These compounds are often referred to as "antinutrients" because they can interfere with nutrient absorption and irritate the gut lining. When these foods are removed from your diet, your digestive system can function more smoothly and without the stress of processing these potentially irritating substances.

Moreover, the Carnivore Diet's emphasis on easily digestible animal proteins and fats allows your digestive system to work more efficiently. Unlike plant-based foods that contain complex carbohydrates and fibers, animal foods are simpler in their composition and generally require less digestive effort. This means that your body can break down and absorb the nutrients from these foods more quickly and with less strain on the digestive tract. For many people, this results in less bloating, fewer digestive discomforts, and a more regular and predictable bowel movement pattern.

Another important factor to consider is the role of fiber in digestive health. Conventional wisdom has long held that fiber is essential for a healthy digestive system, but the reality is more nuanced. While fiber can be beneficial for some people, particularly in the context of a high-carbohydrate diet, it can also be a source of digestive problems for others. Fiber is indigestible and can cause bloating, gas, and even constipation in some individuals, particularly if their digestive systems are sensitive or compromised. The Carnivore Diet is naturally low in fiber because it eliminates plant foods, and for many people, this reduction in fiber leads to an improvement in digestive symptoms. Without fiber to bulk up stool and irritate the gut lining, digestion can become smoother and more comfortable.

The Carnivore Diet also has the potential to reduce inflammation in the gut. Chronic inflammation of the gut lining, often caused by a combination of dietary irritants and a disrupted gut microbiome, can lead to a range of digestive issues, including leaky gut syndrome, IBS, and even autoimmune conditions. By removing foods that contribute to gut inflammation—such as grains, sugars, and processed foods—the Carnivore Diet allows the gut to heal. Additionally, the diet's focus on anti-inflammatory animal fats, particularly those rich in omega-3 fatty acids, can further support the reduction of gut inflammation and promote a healthier digestive environment.

Gut health is closely linked to the balance of bacteria in your digestive tract, known as the gut microbiome. While a diet high in fiber is often recommended to support a healthy microbiome, it's important to recognize that the Carnivore Diet can also have a positive impact on your gut bacteria. The absence of sugars and processed carbohydrates, which can feed harmful bacteria and yeast, creates a less hospitable environment for these unwanted microbes. Meanwhile, the high-quality proteins and fats from animal foods provide the nutrients that beneficial bacteria need to thrive. Some people on the Carnivore Diet report an initial period of adjustment as their gut microbiome adapts to the new way of eating, but over time, many experience a more balanced and resilient gut microbiome, leading to improved digestion and overall gut health.

Furthermore, the Carnivore Diet's ability to support a healthy gut is reflected in the reduction of symptoms in individuals with more serious digestive conditions. Many people with conditions such as Crohn's disease, ulcerative colitis, or severe IBS find that their symptoms improve significantly when they switch to a Carnivore Diet. This can be attributed to the diet's elimination of common food triggers, its anti-inflammatory effects, and its support for gut healing. By giving the digestive system, a break from foods that aggravate these conditions, the Carnivore Diet allows the gut lining to repair and strengthens, leading to a reduction in symptoms and a better quality of life.

It's also worth mentioning that improved digestion on the Carnivore Diet isn't just about the absence of negative symptoms; it's also about how well your body can absorb and utilize the nutrients you consume. Animal-based foods are not only easier to digest, but they also offer nutrients in their most bioavailable forms. This means that your body can absorb and use these nutrients more effectively, leading to better overall health. For example, the heme iron found in red meat is more easily absorbed than the non-heme iron found in plant foods, and the vitamin A in liver is already in its active form, unlike the beta-carotene in vegetables, which must be converted by your body into usable vitamin A.

CHAPTER 3: THE 90-DAY SCIENTIFIC FOOD PROTOCOL

OVERVIEW OF THE 90-DAY PLAN

Embarking on a 90-day Carnivore Diet plan is a powerful commitment to transforming your health and well-being. This structured approach allows you to fully immerse yourself in the diet, providing enough time to experience the profound benefits it can offer. The 90-day period is carefully designed to help you transition smoothly into the diet, overcome initial challenges, and fully adapt to this way of eating. By the end of the three months, you should have a clear understanding of how the Carnivore Diet impacts your body, mind, and overall health.

Phase 1: Transition and Adaptation (Weeks 1-3)
The first phase of the 90-day plan focuses on transitioning your body from its previous diet to the Carnivore Diet. This phase can be challenging as your body adjusts to the elimination of carbohydrates and the introduction of a diet that is exclusively animal-based. During this period, it's common to experience some initial discomforts, such as carb withdrawal symptoms, changes in digestion, or fluctuations in energy levels. However, these are temporary and are part of your body's natural process of adapting to a new metabolic state.

In this phase, you'll focus on the fundamentals of the Carnivore Diet—eating a variety of animal-based foods such as beef, pork, poultry, seafood, and eggs. You'll also eliminate all plant-based foods, including fruits, vegetables, grains, and legumes. The goal is to allow your body to enter ketosis, where it begins to burn fat for fuel instead of glucose. You'll be encouraged to stay hydrated, include adequate salt and electrolytes to prevent imbalances, and eat until you're satisfied without restricting calories.

Phase 2: Stabilization *(Weeks 4-8)*
As you move into the second phase, your body will start to adapt more fully to the Carnivore Diet. The initial challenges of the first few weeks should begin to subside, and you'll likely notice improvements in energy levels, mental clarity, and digestion. This phase is about stabilizing your body in its new metabolic state and continuing to refine your approach to the diet.

During these weeks, you may begin to see more tangible benefits, such as weight loss, reduced inflammation, and improved body composition. Your appetite may become more regulated, and cravings for non-carnivore foods should diminish significantly. You'll also become more attuned to your body's signals, learning when to eat and how much to eat based on your natural hunger and fullness cues rather than external factors like meal times or portion sizes.

This phase is also an excellent time to experiment with different cuts of meat, organ meats, and other animal products to ensure you're getting a broad spectrum of nutrients. You may also start to notice improvements in your physical performance if you're engaged in regular exercise, as your body becomes more efficient at using fat and protein for energy and muscle repair.

Phase 3: Optimization and Long-Term Strategy (Weeks 9-12)
The final phase of the 90-day plan focuses on optimizing your results and setting the stage for long-term success. By this point, you should be fully adapted to the Carnivore Diet, and many of the initial challenges will be a thing of the past. This phase is about fine-tuning your diet to maximize the benefits and determine how to best sustain this way of eating beyond the 90-day period.

In these weeks, you'll evaluate your progress and make any necessary adjustments. This could involve tweaking your food choices, experimenting with meal timing (such as incorporating intermittent fasting), or increasing your focus on nutrient-dense foods like organ meats. You'll also assess how the diet has impacted various aspects of your health, including weight, body composition, energy levels, mental clarity, digestion, and overall well-being.

Additionally, this phase is an opportunity to reflect on how the Carnivore Diet fits into your lifestyle and whether you want to continue with it long-term. For some, the 90-day plan may lead to a permanent shift in eating habits, while others may choose to integrate some plant-based foods back into their diet in a more controlled manner. The key is to understand what works best for you and to create a sustainable approach that supports your health goals.

Throughout the 90-day plan, you'll be encouraged to track your progress, whether through journaling, taking photos, or monitoring changes in how you feel. This will not only help you stay motivated but also provide valuable insights into how your body responds to the Carnivore Diet over time.

SETTING YOUR GOALS: WHAT TO EXPECT IN 90 DAYS

As you embark on the 90-day Carnivore Diet plan, setting clear, realistic goals is essential for maximizing your success and staying motivated throughout the journey. Whether you're aiming for weight loss, improved mental clarity, enhanced energy levels, or better overall health, defining what you want to achieve will help guide your efforts and keep you focused.

What to Expect in the First 30 Days

The first 30 days of the Carnivore Diet are all about adaptation. During this period, your body is transitioning from its previous diet to a high-protein, low-carb, fat-focused approach. As your body adjusts, you may experience some initial discomfort, such as carb withdrawal symptoms, digestive changes, or fluctuations in energy levels. These are normal and typically subside as your body becomes more efficient at using fat for fuel.
In the first month, your primary goals might include:

- **Adapting to the Diet:** Focus on consistency and making the transition as smooth as possible. This might involve gradually reducing carb intake before fully committing to the diet or ensuring you're consuming enough electrolytes to prevent imbalances.
- **Establishing New Eating Habits:** Begin to establish a routine that works for you, such as meal planning, trying new recipes, and finding what types of animal-based foods you enjoy most.
- **Monitoring Early Changes:** Pay attention to how your body is responding to the diet. This includes tracking weight changes, energy levels, digestion, and any improvements in symptoms if you're managing a specific health condition.

By the end of the first 30 days, you should start to feel more comfortable with the diet and notice the beginnings of some of the benefits, such as stabilized energy levels, reduced cravings, and improved digestion.

What to Expect in the Second 30 Days

The next 30 days, from weeks 5 to 8, are about stabilization and deeper adaptation. By now, your body should be more accustomed to burning fat for energy, and many of the initial challenges should be behind you. This is the period where you start to see more significant and noticeable changes in your body and overall well-being.
During this phase, your goals might include:

- **Enhancing Physical Performance:** If one of your goals is related to fitness, this is the time to start noticing improvements in strength, endurance, and recovery. You may find that your workouts feel more energized and that you're able to push yourself further without the same level of fatigue you experienced before.
- **Refining Your Diet:** As you become more comfortable with the Carnivore Diet, you might start experimenting with different cuts of meat, incorporating organ meats, or adjusting your fat intake to optimize your energy levels and overall health.
- **Monitoring Health Markers:** If you're tracking specific health markers, such as blood pressure, cholesterol levels, or inflammation, this is the time to assess any improvements. Many people find that conditions like high blood pressure, insulin resistance, and joint pain begin to improve significantly during this phase.

By the end of the second 30 days, you should feel more confident in your dietary choices and begin to see more substantial changes in your body composition, energy levels, and overall health.

What to Expect in the Final 30 Days

The last 30 days of the 90-day plan are focused on optimization and setting the stage for long-term success. By this point, your body should be fully adapted to the Carnivore Diet, and you'll be experiencing the diet's full range of benefits. This phase is about fine-tuning your approach and making any necessary adjustments to ensure that you continue to thrive on the diet.

Your goals during this phase might include:

- **Achieving Body Composition Goals:** Whether your goal is to lose weight, build muscle, or reduce body fat, the final 30 days are an opportunity to refine your approach and push towards your desired outcomes. You may find that your body is now more responsive to adjustments in your diet and exercise routine, allowing you to make more targeted progress.
- **Sustaining Mental Clarity and Energy Levels:** Continue to monitor your mental clarity and energy levels, making adjustments as needed to maintain consistent performance. This might involve tweaking your meal timing, experimenting with intermittent fasting, or increasing your intake of specific nutrients.
- **Preparing for Long-Term Maintenance:** As you approach the end of the 90-day plan, start thinking about how you want to move forward. Whether you choose to continue with the Carnivore Diet, incorporate other foods, or adopt a more flexible approach, this is the time to plan your long-term strategy. Consider what has worked well for you, what challenges you've faced, and how you can maintain your progress moving forward.

By the end of the 90 days, you should have a deep understanding of how the Carnivore Diet works for your body. You'll have experienced significant changes in your health, energy, and overall well-being, and you'll be equipped with the knowledge and tools to continue your journey, whether that means sticking with the Carnivore Diet or adapting it to suit your individual needs.

90-DAYS COMPLETE MEAL PLAN

WEEK 1: INTRODUCTION TO CARNIVORE BASICS

Day 1
- **Breakfast:** Bacon and Egg Scramble
- **Lunch:** Beef and Bacon Skewers
- **Dinner:** Beef Short Ribs

Day 2
- **Breakfast:** Pork and Egg Breakfast Skillet
- **Lunch:** Grilled Chicken Drumsticks
- **Dinner:** Beef Bone Marrow and Steak

Day 3
- **Breakfast:** Simple Pork Sausage Patties
- **Lunch:** Pan-Fried Chicken Breasts
- **Dinner:** New York Strip Steak with Herb Butter

Day 4
- **Breakfast:** Eggs Benedict Carnivore Style
- **Lunch:** Beef Meatballs
- **Dinner:** Braised Lamb Shanks

Day 5
- **Breakfast:** Omelette with Bacon and Cheese
- **Lunch:** Pork Belly Bites
- **Dinner:** Garlic Butter Pork Tenderloin

Day 6
- **Breakfast:** Steak and Egg Breakfast Bowl
- **Lunch:** Grilled Pork Loin
- **Dinner:** Roasted Lamb with Rosemary

Day 7
- **Breakfast:** Egg and Sausage Muffin Cups
- **Lunch:** Pepper-Crusted Steak
- **Dinner:** Slow-Cooked Brisket

WEEK 2: EXPLORING VARIETY

Day 8
- **Breakfast:** Egg and Sausage Breakfast Skillet
- **Lunch:** Grilled Lamb T-Bone
- **Dinner:** Seared Beef Tips

Day 9
- **Breakfast:** Beef and Egg Scramble
- **Lunch:** Bacon-Wrapped Chicken Breasts
- **Dinner:** Pork Shoulder Roast

Day 10
- **Breakfast:** Mini Egg Frittatas
- **Lunch:** Chicken Breast with Lemon Butter
- **Dinner:** Minted Lamb Stew

Day 11
- **Breakfast:** Soft-Boiled Eggs with Herb Butter
- **Lunch:** Pulled Pork
- **Dinner:** Garlic Butter Lamb Chops

Day 12
- **Breakfast:** Creamy Egg Salad
- **Lunch:** Herbed Chicken Wings
- **Dinner:** Roasted Sea Bass

Day 13
- **Breakfast:** Spicy Deviled Eggs
- **Lunch:** Pork Sausage Patties
- **Dinner:** Grilled Lamb Skewers

Day 14
- **Breakfast:** Salmon and Egg Casserole
- **Lunch:** Beef Liver and Onion
- **Dinner:** Chicken and Bacon Skewers

WEEK 3: ENHANCING NUTRIENT DENSITY

Day 15
- **Breakfast:** Omelette with Bacon and Cheese
- **Lunch:** Pan-Seared Pork Medallions
- **Dinner:** Beef Shank with Garlic Butter

Day 16
- **Breakfast:** Bacon and Egg Scramble
- **Lunch:** Turkey and Egg Bake
- **Dinner:** Lamb Meatballs

Day 17
- **Breakfast:** Steak and Egg Breakfast Bowl
- **Lunch:** Grilled Pork Loin
- **Dinner:** Duck Breast with Black Pepper Butter

Day 18
- **Breakfast:** Mini Egg Frittatas
- **Lunch:** Pork Belly Bites
- **Dinner:** Spicy Chicken Wings

Day 19
- **Breakfast:** Soft-Boiled Eggs with Herb Butter

- **Lunch:** Lamb with Thyme and Lemon
- **Dinner:** Crispy Pork Rinds

Day 20
- **Breakfast:** Cheesy Egg-Stuffed Meatballs
- **Lunch:** Pan-Fried Chicken Breasts
- **Dinner:** Butter-Basted Turkey Thighs

Day 21
- **Breakfast:** Beef and Egg Stir-Fry
- **Lunch:** Baked Chicken Drumsticks
- **Dinner:** Duck Confit with Garlic and Thyme

WEEK 4: REFINED CARNIVORE EXPERIENCE

Day 22
- **Breakfast:** Eggs Benedict Carnivore Style
- **Lunch:** Grilled Lamb T-Bone
- **Dinner:** Pork Shoulder Roast

Day 23
- **Breakfast:** Creamy Egg Salad
- **Lunch:** Seared Beef Tips
- **Dinner:** Cajun-Spiced Duck Breast

Day 24
- **Breakfast:** Egg and Sausage Muffin Cups
- **Lunch:** Bacon-Wrapped Pork Chops
- **Dinner:** Grilled Oysters

Day 25
- **Breakfast:** Omelette with Bacon and Cheese
- **Lunch:** Pulled Pork
- **Dinner:** Beef Bone Marrow and Steak

Day 26
- **Breakfast:** Bacon and Egg Scramble
- **Lunch:** Grilled Shrimp Skewers
- **Dinner:** Roasted Duck Breast with Sage

Day 27
- **Breakfast:** Steak and Egg Breakfast Bowl
- **Lunch:** Turkey Thighs with Sage Butter
- **Dinner:** Pepper-Crusted Steak

Day 28
- **Breakfast:** Mini Egg Frittatas
- **Lunch:** Pan-Seared Pork Medallions
- **Dinner:** Minted Lamb Stew

WEEK 5: OPTIMIZING NUTRIENT INTAKE

Day 29
- **Breakfast:** Bacon and Egg Scramble
- **Lunch:** Garlic Butter Pork Tenderloin
- **Dinner:** Braised Lamb Shanks

Day 30
- **Breakfast:** Steak and Egg Breakfast Bowl
- **Lunch:** Beef Liver and Onion
- **Dinner:** Cajun-Spiced Shrimp

Day 31
- **Breakfast:** Soft-Boiled Eggs with Herb Butter
- **Lunch:** Pork and Egg Breakfast Skillet
- **Dinner:** Slow-Cooked Brisket

Day 32
- **Breakfast:** Omelette with Bacon and Cheese
- **Lunch:** Chicken Breast with Lemon Butter
- **Dinner:** Roasted Sea Bass

Day 33
- **Breakfast:** Creamy Egg Salad
- **Lunch:** Grilled Lamb Skewers
- **Dinner:** Crispy Duck Skin Chips

Day 34
- **Breakfast:** Mini Egg Frittatas
- **Lunch:** Herbed Turkey Cutlets
- **Dinner:** Lamb with Thyme and Lemon

Day 35
- **Breakfast:** Beef and Egg Stir-Fry
- **Lunch:** Grilled Chicken Drumsticks
- **Dinner:** Duck Breast with Rosemary Butter

WEEK 6: MASTERING THE DIET

Day 36
- **Breakfast:** Spicy Deviled Eggs
- **Lunch:** Pulled Pork
- **Dinner:** Grilled Oysters

Day 37
- **Breakfast:** Soft-Boiled Eggs with Herb Butter
- **Lunch:** Braised Lamb Shanks
- **Dinner:** Seared Beef Tips

Day 38
- **Breakfast:** Bacon and Egg Scramble
- **Lunch:** Spicy Turkey Meatballs
- **Dinner:** Butter-Basted Lobster Tails

Day 39
- **Breakfast:** Steak and Egg Breakfast Bowl
- **Lunch:** Beef Short Ribs
- **Dinner:** Duck Fat Roasted Whole Duck with Thyme

Day 40
- **Breakfast:** Mini Egg Frittatas
- **Lunch:** Pan-Fried Chicken Breasts
- **Dinner:** Lamb Meatballs

Day 41
- **Breakfast:** Cheesy Egg-Stuffed Meatballs
- **Lunch:** Crispy Pork Rinds
- **Dinner:** Pork Shoulder Roast

Day 42
- **Breakfast:** Omelette with Bacon and Cheese
- **Lunch:** Bacon-Wrapped Scallops
- **Dinner:** New York Strip Steak with Herb Butter

WEEK 7: ADVANCED CARNIVORE TECHNIQUES

Day 43
- **Breakfast:** Bacon and Egg Scramble
- **Lunch:** Roasted Chicken Quarters
- **Dinner:** Garlic Butter Lamb Chops

Day 44
- **Breakfast:** Steak and Egg Breakfast Bowl
- **Lunch:** Grilled Pork Loin
- **Dinner:** Minted Lamb Stew

Day 45
- **Breakfast:** Egg and Sausage Muffin Cups
- **Lunch:** Pulled Pork
- **Dinner:** Duck Breast with Black Pepper Butter

Day 46
- **Breakfast:** Soft-Boiled Eggs with Herb Butter
- **Lunch:** Pork Belly Bites
- **Dinner:** Grilled Shrimp Skewers

Day 47
- **Breakfast:** Creamy Egg Salad
- **Lunch:** Lamb with Thyme and Lemon
- **Dinner:** Seared Beef Tips

Day 48
- **Breakfast:** Mini Egg Frittatas
- **Lunch:** Herbed Chicken Wings
- **Dinner:** Beef Meatballs

Day 49
- **Breakfast:** Omelette with Bacon and Cheese
- **Lunch:** Beef and Bacon Skewers
- **Dinner:** Duck Confit with Garlic and Thyme

WEEK 8: FINAL PREPARATIONS

Day 50
- **Breakfast:** Bacon and Egg Scramble
- **Lunch:** Pork Shoulder Roast
- **Dinner:** Cajun-Spiced Duck Breast

Day 51
- **Breakfast:** Steak and Egg Breakfast Bowl
- **Lunch:** Crispy Chicken Wings
- **Dinner:** Roasted Sea Bass

Day 52
- **Breakfast:** Mini Egg Frittatas
- **Lunch:** Seared Beef Tips
- **Dinner:** Minted Lamb Stew

Day 53
- **Breakfast:** Soft-Boiled Eggs with Herb Butter
- **Lunch:** Grilled Pork Loin
- **Dinner:** Butter-Basted Turkey Thighs

Day 54
- **Breakfast:** Creamy Egg Salad
- **Lunch:** Braised Lamb Shanks
- **Dinner:** Bacon-Wrapped Scallops

Day 55
- **Breakfast:** Omelette with Bacon and Cheese
- **Lunch:** Pulled Pork
- **Dinner:** Beef Bone Marrow and Steak

Day 56
- **Breakfast:** Beef and Egg Stir-Fry
- **Lunch:** Grilled Chicken Drumsticks
- **Dinner:** Lamb Meatballs

WEEK 9: PEAK CARNIVORE

Day 57
- **Breakfast:** Egg and Sausage Breakfast Skillet
- **Lunch:** Grilled Lamb Skewers
- **Dinner:** Roasted Duck Breast with Sage

Day 58
- **Breakfast:** Spicy Deviled Eggs
- **Lunch:** Beef Liver and Onion
- **Dinner:** Slow-Cooked Brisket

Day 59
- **Breakfast:** Soft-Boiled Eggs with Herb Butter
- **Lunch:** Pan-Fried Chicken Breasts
- **Dinner:** Garlic Butter Pork Tenderloin

Day 60
- **Breakfast:** Bacon and Egg Scramble
- **Lunch:** Lamb with Thyme and Lemon
- **Dinner:** Crispy Duck Skin Chips

Day 61
- **Breakfast:** Steak and Egg Breakfast Bowl
- **Lunch:** Beef Short Ribs
- **Dinner:** Spicy Garlic Shrimp

Day 62
- **Breakfast:** Creamy Egg Salad
- **Lunch:** Roasted Chicken Quarters
- **Dinner:** Pepper-Crusted Steak

Day 63
- **Breakfast:** Mini Egg Frittatas
- **Lunch:** Herbed Turkey Cutlets
- **Dinner:** Duck Breast with Rosemary Butter

WEEK 10: REFINING YOUR ROUTINE

Day 64
- **Breakfast:** Omelette with Bacon and Cheese
- **Lunch:** Pan-Seared Pork Medallions
- **Dinner:** Minted Lamb Stew

Day 65
- **Breakfast:** Bacon and Egg Scramble
- **Lunch:** Pork and Egg Breakfast Skillet
- **Dinner:** Beef Shank with Garlic Butter

Day 66
- **Breakfast:** Spicy Deviled Eggs
- **Lunch:** Lamb Meatballs
- **Dinner:** Roasted Sea Bass

Day 67
- **Breakfast:** Beef and Egg Stir-Fry
- **Lunch:** Pork Belly Bites
- **Dinner:** Garlic Herb Duck Wings

Day 68
- **Breakfast:** Soft-Boiled Eggs with Herb Butter
- **Lunch:** Pulled Pork
- **Dinner:** Grilled Shrimp Skewers

Day 69
- **Breakfast:** Mini Egg Frittatas
- **Lunch:** Bacon-Wrapped Chicken Breasts
- **Dinner:** Beef and Bacon Skewers

Day 70
- **Breakfast:** Omelette with Bacon and Cheese
- **Lunch:** Grilled Lamb T-Bone
- **Dinner:** Slow-Cooked Brisket

WEEK 11: MASTERING THE CARNIVORE LIFESTYLE

Day 71
- **Breakfast:** Bacon and Egg Scramble
- **Lunch:** Grilled Chicken Drumsticks
- **Dinner:** Garlic Butter Pork Tenderloin

Day 72
- **Breakfast:** Steak and Egg Breakfast Bowl
- **Lunch:** Beef Liver and Onion
- **Dinner:** Duck Fat Roasted Whole Duck with Thyme

Day 73
- **Breakfast:** Egg and Sausage Muffin Cups
- **Lunch:** Pulled Pork
- **Dinner:** Seared Beef Tips

Day 74
- **Breakfast:** Spicy Deviled Eggs
- **Lunch:** Grilled Oysters
- **Dinner:** Pepper-Crusted Steak

Day 75
- **Breakfast:** Soft-Boiled Eggs with Herb Butter
- **Lunch:** Beef Meatballs
- **Dinner:** Lamb with Thyme and Lemon

Day 76
- **Breakfast:** Mini Egg Frittatas
- **Lunch:** Grilled Pork Loin
- **Dinner:** Braised Lamb Shanks

Day 77
- **Breakfast:** Creamy Egg Salad
- **Lunch:** Pan-Fried Chicken Breasts
- **Dinner:** Roasted Duck Breast with Sage

WEEK 12: FINAL STRETCH

Day 78
- **Breakfast:** Bacon and Egg Scramble
- **Lunch:** Pork Shoulder Roast
- **Dinner:** Cajun-Spiced Duck Breast

Day 79
- **Breakfast:** Steak and Egg Breakfast Bowl
- **Lunch:** Pan-Seared Pork Medallions
- **Dinner:** Roasted Sea Bass

Day 80
- **Breakfast:** Soft-Boiled Eggs with Herb Butter
- **Lunch:** Grilled Lamb T-Bone
- **Dinner:** Spicy Garlic Shrimp

Day 81
- **Breakfast:** Egg and Sausage Muffin Cups
- **Lunch:** Beef Short Ribs
- **Dinner:** Lamb Meatballs

Day 82
- **Breakfast:** Spicy Deviled Eggs
- **Lunch:** Grilled Pork Loin
- **Dinner:** Duck Breast with Rosemary Butter

Day 83
- **Breakfast:** Bacon and Egg Scramble
- **Lunch:** Beef Liver and Onion
- **Dinner:** Garlic Butter Pork Tenderloin

Day 84
- **Breakfast:** Creamy Egg Salad
- **Lunch:** Roasted Chicken Quarters
- **Dinner:** Pepper-Crusted Steak

WEEK 13: FINISHING STRONG

Day 85
- **Breakfast:** Mini Egg Frittatas
- **Lunch:** Pulled Pork
- **Dinner:** Minted Lamb Stew

Day 86
- **Breakfast:** Bacon and Egg Scramble
- **Lunch:** Crispy Chicken Wings
- **Dinner:** Beef Bone Marrow and Steak

Day 87
- **Breakfast:** Steak and Egg Breakfast Bowl
- **Lunch:** Pork and Egg Breakfast Skillet
- **Dinner:** Grilled Shrimp Skewers

Day 88
- **Breakfast:** Soft-Boiled Eggs with Herb Butter
- **Lunch:** Lamb Meatballs
- **Dinner:** Duck Confit with Garlic and Thyme

Day 89
- **Breakfast:** Spicy Deviled Eggs
- **Lunch:** Seared Beef Tips
- **Dinner:** Braised Lamb Shanks

Day 90
- **Breakfast:** Omelette with Bacon and Cheese
- **Lunch:** Beef and Bacon Skewers
- **Dinner:** Roasted Sea Bass

PART 2: CARNIVORE DIET RECIPES BY FOOD CATEGORY

Welcome to Part 2 of your Carnivore Diet journey, where we dive into the delicious and diverse world of animal-based recipes. In this chapter, you'll find 90 carefully curated recipes organized by food category, designed to make your Carnivore Diet both enjoyable and sustainable. Whether you're craving a hearty steak, flavorful seafood, or nutrient-packed organ meats, there's something here for every palate. These recipes are crafted to be simple, yet satisfying, allowing you to savor the full range of flavors and benefits that the Carnivore Diet has to offer. Let's explore the endless possibilities of carnivore cuisine together!

CHAPTER 6: MEAT RECIPES

BEEF RECIPES

BEEF AND BACON SKEWERS RECIPE

Preparation Time: 10 minutes
Cooking Time: 15 minutes
Portions: 1 person
Ingredients:

- 6 oz beef sirloin, cut into 1-inch cubes
- 3 slices of bacon, cut in half
- 1 tbsp butter, melted
- 1/2 tsp sea salt
- 1/4 tsp black pepper
- 1/4 tsp garlic powder

Instructions:

1. Preheat your grill or stovetop grill pan to medium-high heat. Season with sea salt, black pepper, and garlic powder. Toss the beef cubes to ensure they are evenly coated. Take a piece of beef and wrap it with half a slice of bacon. Thread the bacon-wrapped beef onto a skewer. Repeat the process until all the beef cubes are used.
2. Brush the skewers with melted butter on all sides. Place them on the preheated grill or grill pan. Cook for about 3-4 minutes on each side, turning the skewers to ensure even cooking. The bacon should be crispy, and the beef should be cooked to your desired level of doneness. Once cooked, remove the skewers from the grill and let them rest for a minute.

Nutritional Values: Calories: 500 kcal; **Protein:** 35g; **Fat:** 40g; **Carbohydrates:** 0g; **Sodium:** 1200mg

BEEF BONE MARROW AND STEAK RECIPE

Preparation Time: 10 minutes
Cooking Time: 20 minutes
Portions: 1 person
Ingredients:

- 8 oz ribeye steak
- 1 beef bone marrow (cut lengthwise)
- 1 tbsp butter, melted
- 1/2 tsp sea salt and 1/4 tsp black pepper

Instructions:

1. Preheat your oven to 450°F (230°C) for the bone marrow. Season the ribeye steak with sea salt and black pepper on both sides. Let it sit at room temperature while preparing the bone marrow.
2. Place the bone marrow halves on a baking sheet, cut side up. Roast in the preheated oven for about 15 minutes, or until the marrow is soft and bubbly. While the bone marrow is roasting, heat a grill pan or skillet over medium-high heat. Brush the ribeye steak with melted butter on both sides. Cook for about 4-5 minutes on each side for medium-rare. Once done, carefully remove it from the oven. Serve the steak on a plate, with the roasted bone marrow on the side.

Nutritional Values: Calories:750 kcal; **Protein:** 50g; **Fat:** 60g; **Carbohydrates:** 0g; **Sodium:** 800mg

BEEF LIVER AND ONION RECIPE

Preparation Time: 10 minutes
Cooking Time: 15 minutes
Portions: 1 person
Ingredients:
- 6 oz beef liver, sliced into thin strips
- 1 small onion, thinly sliced (optional and sparingly used)
- 2 tbsp beef tallow (or butter)
- 1/2 tsp sea salt
- 1/4 tsp black pepper

Instructions:
1. Thinly slice the beef liver into strips. If using, slice the onion thinly. Keep the onion portion small as it is optional and sparingly used on the carnivore diet. Heat 1 tablespoon of beef tallow in a skillet over medium heat. Add the sliced onion to the skillet and cook until they are soft and slightly caramelized, about 5 minutes.
2. Remove the onion from the skillet and set aside. In the same skillet, add the remaining tablespoon of beef tallow. Increase the heat to medium-high and add the beef liver slices to the skillet. Cook the liver for 2-3 minutes on each side until browned but still slightly pink in the center. Do not overcook, as liver can become tough.
3. Season with sea salt and black pepper while cooking.
4. Once the liver is cooked, return the onions to the skillet and mix them with the liver. Cook for an additional 1-2 minutes to combine the flavors. Serve immediately.

Nutritional Values: Calories: 350kcal; **Protein:** 25g; **Fat:** 25g; **Carbohydrates:** 3g; **Sodium:** 600mg

BEEF MEATBALLS RECIPE

Preparation Time: 10 minutes
Cooking Time: 15 minutes
Portions: 1 person
Ingredients:
- 8 oz ground beef
- 1 egg
- 1/2 tsp sea salt
- 1/4 tsp black pepper
- 1/4 tsp garlic powder
- 1 tbsp beef tallow (or butter) for cooking

Instructions:
1. In a mixing bowl, combine the ground beef, egg, sea salt, black pepper, and garlic powder. Mix well until all ingredients are fully incorporated. Using your hands, form the mixture into small meatballs, about 1 inch in diameter. This recipe should make approximately 6-8 meatballs, depending on size.
2. Heat the beef tallow (or butter) in a skillet over medium heat. Once the tallow is hot, add the meatballs to the skillet, being careful not to overcrowd them. Cook the meatballs for about 8-10 minutes, turning them occasionally to ensure they are browned on all sides and cooked through. If needed, reduce the heat slightly to avoid burning and to ensure the meatballs cook evenly.
3. Once fully cooked, remove the meatballs from the skillet and let them rest for a minute. Serve immediately as a main dish or with a side of your choice that fits within the carnivore diet.

Nutritional Values: Calories: 450kcal; **Protein:** 30g; **Fat:** 35g; **Carbohydrates:** 0g; **Sodium:** 700mg

BEEF SHORT RIBS RECIPE

Preparation Time: 10 minutes
Cooking Time: 2.5 hours
Portions: 1 person
Ingredients:
- 1 lb beef short ribs
- 1 tsp sea salt
- 1/2 tsp black pepper
- 1/2 tsp garlic powder
- 1/2 cup bone broth
- 1 tbsp butter (optional for serving)

Instructions:
1. Preheat your oven to 300°F (150°C). Season the beef short ribs on all sides with sea salt, black pepper, and garlic powder. In a large oven-safe skillet or Dutch oven, heat the skillet over medium-high heat. Add the short ribs and sear them on all sides until browned, about 2-3 minutes per side. Once seared, remove the short ribs and set them aside.
2. In the same skillet, pour in the bone broth and bring it to a simmer. Return the short ribs to the skillet, ensuring they are partially submerged in the broth. Cover the skillet with a lid or foil and transfer it to the preheated oven. Let the short ribs braise in the oven for about 2.5 hours, or until the meat is tender and easily pulls away from the bone. Check halfway through cooking to ensure there is enough liquid; add more bone broth if necessary. Once cooked, carefully remove the short ribs from the oven. Serve the ribs hot, optionally with some of the braising liquid as a sauce.

Nutritional Values: Calories: 850kcal; **Protein:** 50g; **Fat:** 70g; **Carbohydrates:** 0g; **Sodium:** 900mg

GROUND BEEF AND EGG SCRAMBLE RECIPE

Preparation Time: 5 minutes
Cooking Time: 10 minutes
Portions: 1 person
Ingredients:
- 6 oz ground beef
- 2 large eggs
- 1 tbsp butter
- 1/2 tsp sea salt
- 1/4 tsp black pepper
- 1/4 tsp garlic powder (optional)

Instructions:
1. Crack the eggs into a bowl and whisk them together until well combined. Set aside. Heat a skillet over medium heat and add the butter. Once the butter has melted, add the ground beef to the skillet. Season the beef with sea salt, black pepper, and garlic powder (if using). Cook the ground beef, breaking it up with a spatula, until it is fully browned and cooked through, about 5-7 minutes. Once the ground beef is cooked, reduce the heat to low. Pour the whisked eggs into the skillet with beef. Stir continuously, gently scrambling the eggs and mixing them with the beef.
2. Cook for about 2-3 minutes, or until the eggs are fully cooked and scrambled to your liking. Once the eggs are cooked, remove the skillet from heat. Serve the ground beef and egg scramble immediately.

Nutritional Values: Calories: 450 kcal; **Protein:** 35g; **Fat:** 35g; **Carbohydrates:** 0g; **Sodium:** 600mg

NEW YORK STRIP STEAK WITH HERB BUTTER RECIPE

Preparation Time: 5 minutes
Cooking Time: 10-12 minutes
Portions: 1 person
Ingredients:

- 8 oz New York strip steak
- 2 tbsp butter, softened
- 1/2 tsp sea salt
- 1/4 tsp black pepper
- 1/4 tsp garlic powder

Instructions:

1. In a small bowl, combine the softened butter with the chopped parsley and garlic powder. Mix well until the herbs and garlic are evenly distributed throughout the butter. Set the herb butter aside.
2. Pat the New York strip steak dry with paper towels to ensure a good sear. Season both sides of the steak with sea salt and black pepper. Heat a skillet over medium-high heat until it is very hot. Add the seasoned steak to the hot skillet. Let it cook undisturbed for 3-4 minutes on the first side to develop a good sear. Flip the steak and cook for another 3-4 minutes on the other side for medium-rare. Adjust the cooking time according to your preferred level of doneness.
3. In the last minute of cooking, place the prepared herb butter on top of the steak. Allow the butter to melt and baste the steak as it finishes cooking. Remove the steak from the skillet and let it rest for a couple of minutes before serving. Slice the steak against the grain and drizzle any remaining herb butter from the skillet over the top.

Nutritional Values: Calories: 550 kcal; **Protein:** 40g; **Fat:** 45g; **Carbohydrates:** 0g; **Sodium:** 700mg

PEPPER-CRUSTED STEAK RECIPE

Preparation Time: 5 minutes
Cooking Time: 10-12 minutes
Portions: 1 person
Ingredients:

- 8 oz ribeye steak
- 1 tbsp black peppercorns, coarsely crushed
- 1/2 tsp sea salt
- 1 tbsp butter
- 1 tbsp beef tallow (or additional butter)

Instructions:

1. Pat the ribeye steak dry with paper towels to ensure a good sear. Spread the coarsely crushed black peppercorns evenly on a plate. Press both sides of the steak into the crushed peppercorns to create a crust. Season both sides of the steak with sea salt. Place a heavy-bottomed skillet over medium-high heat. Add the beef tallow to the skillet and allow it to heat until shimmering. Carefully place the pepper-crusted steak into the hot skillet.
2. Sear the steak for about 3-4 minutes on the first side without moving it, to develop a crust. Flip the steak and add the tablespoon of butter to the skillet. Using a spoon, baste the steak with the melted butter as it cooks for another 3-4 minutes for medium-rare. Once cooked to your liking, remove the steak from the skillet and place it on a cutting board. Let the steak rest for about 5 minutes to allow the juices to redistribute. Slice against the grain and serve immediately, drizzling any remaining pan juices over the slices.

Nutritional Values: Calories: 600 kcal; **Protein:** 45g; **Fat:** 48g; **Carbohydrates:** 1g; **Sodium:** 800mg

SEARED BEEF TIPS RECIPE

Preparation Time: 5 minutes
Cooking Time: 10 minutes
Portions: 1 person
Ingredients:
- 8 oz beef tips (sirloin or tenderloin)
- 1 tbsp beef tallow (or butter)
- 1/2 tsp sea salt
- 1/4 tsp black pepper
- 1/4 tsp garlic powder
- 1 tsp fresh thyme leaves (optional)

Instructions:
1. Pat the beef tips dry with paper towels to remove excess moisture. Season the beef tips with sea salt, black pepper, and garlic powder, ensuring they are evenly coated. Place a heavy-bottomed skillet (such as cast iron) over medium-high heat. Add the beef tallow (or butter) to the skillet and allow it to melt and heat until it begins to shimmer.
2. Add the seasoned beef tips to the hot skillet in a single layer, ensuring they are not overcrowded. Sear the beef tips for about 2-3 minutes on the first side, allowing them to develop a rich, brown crust. Flip the beef tips and sear the other side for an additional 2-3 minutes, or until they reach your desired level of doneness. If using, add the fresh thyme leaves to the skillet during the last minute of cooking. Stir the thyme through the beef tips, allowing its aroma to infuse the meat.
3. Once cooked, remove the beef tips from the skillet and let them rest for a minute. Serve immediately.

Nutritional Values: Calories: 400 kcal; **Protein:** 35g; **Fat:** 30g; **Carbohydrates:** 0g; **Sodium:** 600mg

SLOW-COOKED BRISKET RECIPE

Preparation Time: 10 minutes
Cooking Time: 6-8 hours
Portions: 1 person
Ingredients:
- 1 lb beef brisket
- 1 tsp sea salt
- 1/2 tsp black pepper
- 1/2 tsp garlic powder
- 1/2 cup bone broth

Instructions:
1. Pat the beef brisket dry with paper towels to remove excess moisture. Rub the brisket all over with sea salt, black pepper, garlic powder, and onion powder (if using), ensuring an even coating.
2. Heat a skillet over medium-high heat and sear the brisket on all sides until browned, about 2-3 minutes per side. Once seared, remove the brisket from the skillet. Place the seasoned (and seared, if applicable) brisket in a slow cooker. Pour the bone broth over the brisket to keep it moist during cooking. Cover the slow cooker with a lid and cook on low for 6-8 hours, or until the brisket is tender and easily pulls apart with a fork. Once the brisket is cooked, carefully remove it from the slow cooker and let it rest for a few minutes. Slice or shred the brisket and drizzle some of the cooking juices from the slow cooker over the meat for added flavor. Serve immediately.

Nutritional Values: Calories: 800 kcal; **Protein:** 60g; **Fat:** 60g; **Carbohydrates:** 0g; **Sodium:** 800mg

PORK RECIPES

BACON-WRAPPED PORK CHOPS RECIPE

Preparation Time: 5 minutes
Cooking Time: 20 minutes
Portions: 1 person
Ingredients:
- 1 pork chop (approximately 6-8 oz)
- 2 slices of bacon
- 1/2 tsp sea salt
- 1/4 tsp black pepper
- 1 tbsp butter (optional)

Instructions:
1. Preheat your oven to 375°F (190°C). Season the pork chop on both sides with sea salt and black pepper. Take the two slices of bacon and wrap them around the pork chop, securing the ends with toothpicks if necessary. Heat a skillet over medium-high heat and add the butter. Once the butter has melted and the skillet is hot, add the bacon-wrapped pork chop. Sear the pork chop for 2-3 minutes on each side, or until the bacon is browned and crispy.
2. After searing, transfer the pork chop to an oven-safe dish or keep it in the oven-safe skillet. Place the dish or skillet in the preheated oven and bake for 15 minutes, or until the pork chop is cooked through and reaches an internal temperature of 145°F (63°C). Once cooked, remove the pork chop from the oven and let it rest for a few minutes. Remove the toothpicks if used and serve the bacon-wrapped pork chop immediately.

Nutritional Values: Calories: 500 kcal; **Protein:** 40g; **Fat:** 40g; **Carbohydrates:** 0g; **Sodium:** 1000mg

CARNIVORE PORK BELLY BITES RECIPE

Preparation Time: 5 minutes
Cooking Time: 25-30 minutes
Portions: 1 person
Ingredients:
- 8 oz pork belly, cut into bite-sized pieces
- 1/2 tsp sea salt
- 1/4 tsp black pepper
- 1 tbsp butter or beef tallow (optional, for extra crispiness)

Instructions:
1. Preheat your oven to 400°F (200°C). Cut the pork belly into bite-sized pieces, ensuring they are roughly uniform in size for even cooking. Season with sea salt, black pepper, and garlic powder (optional). Heat a skillet over medium-high heat and add the butter or beef tallow. Once the fat is hot, add the pork belly pieces to the skillet and sear them for 2-3 minutes on each side until they are browned and crispy. Remove the pork belly and place on a baking sheet lined with parchment paper. Place the baking sheet with the pork belly bites in the preheated oven. Roast for 20-25 minutes.
2. Remove the pork belly bites from the oven and let them rest for a minute to allow any excess fat to drain off.

Nutritional Values: Calories: 600 kcal; **Protein:** 20g; **Fat:** 55g; **Carbohydrates:** 0g; **Sodium:** 700mg

CRISPY PORK RINDS RECIPE

Preparation Time: 10 minutes
Cooking Time: 2-3 hours (including cooling time)
Portions: 1 person
Ingredients:
- 4 oz pork skin (pork rind)
- 1/2 tsp sea salt
- 1/4 tsp garlic powder (optional)
- 1/4 tsp black pepper (optional)

Instructions:
1. Preheat your oven to 250°F (120°C). Pat the pork skin dry with paper towels to remove any excess moisture. This step is crucial for achieving a crispy texture. Lightly season the pork skin with sea salt. If you desire additional flavor, you can also add garlic powder and black pepper at this stage.
2. Place the seasoned pork skin pieces on a baking sheet lined with parchment paper, ensuring they are evenly spaced and not overlapping. Bake the pork skin in the preheated oven for 1.5 to 2 hours, or until the skin is golden brown and crispy.
3. Check the pork rinds occasionally to ensure they do not burn. They should puff up and become crispy as they bake. Once the pork rinds are crispy, remove them from the oven and let them cool completely on the baking sheet.

Nutritional Values: Calories: 300 kcal; **Protein:** 20g; **Fat:** 25g; **Carbohydrates:** 0g; **Sodium:** 500mg

GARLIC BUTTER PORK TENDERLOIN RECIPE

Preparation Time: 10 minutes
Cooking Time: 20-25 minutes
Portions: 1 person
Ingredients:
- 8 oz pork tenderloin
- 2 tbsp butter, softened
- 1 garlic clove, minced (or 1/2 tsp garlic powder)
- 1/2 tsp sea salt
- 1/4 tsp black pepper
- 1/2 tsp fresh thyme or rosemary (optional)

Instructions:
1. Preheat your oven to 375°F (190°C). Pat the pork tenderloin dry with paper towels. In a small bowl, mix the softened butter with minced garlic (or garlic powder), sea salt, black pepper, and thyme or rosemary (if using). Rub the garlic butter mixture all over the pork tenderloin, ensuring it is evenly coated on all sides. Heat an oven-safe skillet over medium-high heat. Once hot, add the pork tenderloin to the skillet and sear it for 2-3 minutes on each side until it develops a golden-brown crust.
2. Transfer the skillet with the seared pork tenderloin to the preheated oven. Roast the pork tenderloin for 15-20 minutes, or until it reaches an internal temperature of 145°F (63°C) for medium-rare. Baste the pork with the melted garlic butter from the skillet halfway through the cooking time for extra flavor.
3. Once cooked, remove the pork tenderloin from the oven and let it rest for 5 minutes before slicing. Slice the pork tenderloin into medallions and drizzle with any remaining garlic butter from the skillet. Serve immediately.

Nutritional Values: Calories: 400 kcal; **Protein:** 35g; **Fat:** 30g; **Carbohydrates:** 0g; **Sodium:** 800mg

GRILLED PORK LOIN RECIPE

Preparation Time: 5 minutes
Cooking Time: 15-20 minutes
Portions: 1 person
Ingredients:
- 8 oz pork loin
- 1 tbsp olive oil or melted butter
- 1/2 tsp sea salt
- 1/4 tsp black pepper
- 1/4 tsp garlic powder (optional)

Instructions:
1. Preheat your grill to medium-high heat. Pat the pork loin dry with paper towels to remove any excess moisture. Rub the pork loin with olive oil or melted butter, ensuring it is evenly coated. Season the pork loin on all sides with sea salt, black pepper, garlic powder, and paprika (optional). Place the seasoned pork loin on the preheated grill. Grill the pork loin for 6-8 minutes on the first side without moving it, to develop good grill marks.
2. Flip the pork loin and grill for an additional 6-8 minutes on the other side, or until the internal temperature reaches 145°F (63°C) for medium-rare.
3. Once the pork loin is cooked, remove it from the grill and let it rest for 5 minutes before slicing. Slice the pork loin into medallions and serve immediately.

Nutritional Values: Calories: 350 kcal; **Protein:** 30g; **Fat:** 25g; **Carbohydrates:** 0g; **Sodium:** 600mg

PAN-SEARED PORK MEDALLIONS RECIPE

Preparation Time: 5 minutes
Cooking Time: 10 minutes
Portions: 1 person
Ingredients:
- 6 oz pork medallions (sliced from pork tenderloin)
- 1 tbsp ghee
- 1/2 tsp sea salt
- 1/4 tsp black pepper
- 1/2 tsp fresh rosemary, finely chopped (optional)
- 1 garlic clove, crushes

Instructions:
1. Pat the pork medallions dry with paper towels to remove any excess moisture. Season the medallions on both sides with sea salt, black pepper, and fresh rosemary (if using). Heat a skillet over medium-high heat and add the ghee. Once the ghee has melted and is hot, add the crushed garlic clove to the skillet and sauté for about 30 seconds to infuse the ghee with garlic flavor.
2. Add the seasoned pork medallions to the skillet, making sure they are spaced apart. Sear the medallions for 3-4 minutes on the first side, without moving them, to develop a golden-brown crust.
3. Flip the medallions and sear for an additional 3-4 minutes on the other side, or until the internal temperature reaches 145°F (63°C) for medium-rare.
4. Once cooked, remove the pork medallions from the skillet and let them rest for 2-3 minutes. Discard the garlic clove and serve the medallions hot, drizzling any remaining ghee from the skillet over the top.

Nutritional Values: Calories: 350 kcal; **Protein:** 30g; **Fat:** 25g; **Carbohydrates:** 0g; **Sodium:** 600mg

PORK AND EGG BREAKFAST SKILLET RECIPE

Preparation Time: 5 minutes
Cooking Time: 10 minutes
Portions: 1 person
Ingredients:
- 4 oz ground pork (or small pork sausage, crumbled)
- 2 large eggs
- 1 tbsp ghee or butter
- 1/2 tsp sea salt
- 1/4 tsp black pepper
- 1/4 tsp garlic powder (optional)

Instructions:
1. Heat a skillet over medium heat and add the ghee or butter. Add the ground pork or crumbled sausage to the skillet. Season with sea salt, black pepper, and garlic powder (if using). Cook the pork for about 5-6 minutes, breaking it up with a spatula, until it is browned and cooked through.
2. Once the pork is fully cooked, reduce the heat to low. Crack the eggs directly into the skillet with the cooked pork. Stir gently to scramble the eggs with the pork, cooking until the eggs are just set, about 2-3 minutes.
3. Once the eggs are cooked to your liking, remove the skillet from the heat. Serve the pork and egg scramble immediately, straight from the skillet.

Nutritional Values: Calories: 400 kcal; **Protein:** 25g; **Fat:** 35g; **Carbohydrates:** 0g; **Sodium:** 600mg

PORK SHOULDER ROAST RECIPE

Preparation Time: 10 minutes
Cooking Time: 3-4 hours
Portions: 1 person
Ingredients:
- 1 lb pork shoulder
- 1 tsp sea salt
- 1/2 tsp black pepper
- 1/2 tsp garlic powder
- 1/2 tsp paprika (optional)
- 1 tbsp ghee or beef tallow

Instructions:
1. Preheat your oven to 300°F (150°C). Pat the pork shoulder dry with paper towels to remove any excess moisture. In a small bowl, mix the sea salt, black pepper, garlic powder, and paprika (if using). Rub the spice mixture all over the pork shoulder, ensuring it is evenly coated.
2. Heat a large oven-safe skillet or Dutch oven over medium-high heat and add the ghee or beef tallow. Once the fat is hot, add the pork shoulder and sear it on all sides until it is browned, about 3-4 minutes per side.
3. After searing, cover the skillet or Dutch oven with a lid or tightly with aluminum foil. Transfer the covered pork shoulder to the preheated oven. Roast for 3-4 hours, or until the pork is tender and easily pulls apart with a fork. Check periodically to ensure the pork is cooking evenly.
4. Once the pork shoulder is fully cooked, remove it from the oven and let it rest for about 10 minutes. After resting, shred the pork shoulder with a fork or slice it, depending on your preference.

Nutritional Values: Calories: 800kcal; **Protein:** 60g; **Fat:** 60g; **Carbohydrates:** 0g; **Sodium:** 1000mg

PULLED PORK RECIPE

Preparation Time: 10 minutes
Cooking Time: 6-8 hours
Portions: 1 person
Ingredients:
- 1 lb pork butt (also known as pork shoulder)
- 1 tsp sea salt
- 1/2 tsp black pepper
- 1/2 tsp paprika
- 1/2 tsp garlic powder
- 1 tbsp lard

Instructions:
1. Pat the pork butt dry with paper towels to remove any excess moisture. In a small bowl, mix the sea salt, black pepper, paprika, and garlic powder. Rub the spice mixture all over the pork butt, ensuring it is evenly coated. Place the seasoned pork butt in a slow cooker. Cover the slow cooker with a lid and cook on low for 6-8 hours, or until the pork is tender and easily pulls apart with a fork.
2. Once the pork is fully cooked and tender, remove it from the slow cooker. Use two forks to shred the pork into pieces. Return the shredded pork to the slow cooker to mix with the cooking juices, ensuring it stays moist and flavorful.
3. Serve the pulled pork immediately, either on its own or with a side dish that fits within the carnivore diet.

Nutritional Values: Calories: 700 kcal; **Protein:** 50g; **Fat:** 55g; **Carbohydrates:** 0g; **Sodium:** 1200mg

SIMPLE PORK SAUSAGE PATTIES RECIPE

Preparation Time: 5 minutes
Cooking Time: 10 minutes
Portions: 1 person
Ingredients:
- 6 oz ground pork
- 1/2 tsp sea salt
- 1/4 tsp black pepper
- 1/4 tsp dried sage
- 1/4 tsp dried thyme
- 1 tbsp ghee (for cooking)

Instructions:
1. In a mixing bowl, combine the ground pork, sea salt, black pepper, dried sage, and dried thyme. Mix well until all the ingredients are evenly incorporated. Divide the seasoned ground pork into two equal portions. Shape each portion into a patty, pressing them gently to ensure they hold together.
2. Heat a skillet over medium heat and add the ghee. Once the ghee has melted and the skillet is hot, add the sausage patties. Cook the patties for about 4-5 minutes on the first side, until they are browned and cooked through. Flip the patties and cook for an additional 4-5 minutes on the other side, until they reach an internal temperature of 160°F (71°C).
3. Once cooked, remove the sausage patties from the skillet and let them rest for a minute. Serve the sausage patties hot.

Nutritional Values: Calories: 400 kcal; **Protein:** 25g; **Fat:** 35g; **Carbohydrates:** 0g; **Sodium:** 700mg

LAMB RECIPES

BRAISED LAMB SHANKS RECIPE

Preparation Time: 10 minutes
Cooking Time: 2.5 to 3 hours
Portions: 1 person
Ingredients:

- 1 lamb shank (about 12 oz)
- 1 cup beef broth
- 1/2 tsp sea salt
- 1/4 tsp black pepper
- 2 cloves garlic, minced
- 1 tsp fresh rosemary, chopped (or 1/2 tsp dried rosemary)

Instructions:

1. Preheat your oven to 325°F. Season the lamb shank with sea salt and black pepper. In a large oven-safe pot or Dutch oven, heat a small amount of beef broth over medium-high heat. Sear the lamb shank on all sides until browned, about 4-5 minutes per side.
2. Once the lamb is seared, add the minced garlic and chopped rosemary to the pot. Stir for 1 minute to release the flavors. Pour in the beef broth, making sure the lamb shank is partially submerged. Bring the mixture to a simmer, then cover the pot and transfer it to the preheated oven. Braise the lamb shank in the oven for 2.5 to 3 hours, or until the meat is tender and easily pulls away from the bone.
3. Check occasionally to ensure there's enough liquid, adding more broth if needed. Once done, remove the lamb shank from the oven and let it rest for a few minutes before serving.

Nutritional Values: Calories: 600 kcal; **Protein:** 50g; **Fat:** 40g; **Carbohydrates:** 0g; **Sodium:** 900mg

GRILLED LAMB T-BONE RECIPE

Preparation Time: 5 minutes
Cooking Time: 10-12 minutes
Portions: 1 person
Ingredients:

- 1 Lamb T-bone chop (about 8 oz)
- 1/2 tsp sea salt
- 1/4 tsp black pepper
- 1 tsp olive oil
- 1/2 tsp fresh rosemary, chopped (or 1/4 tsp dried rosemary)

Instructions:

1. Preheat your grill to medium-high heat. Brush the lamb T-bone chop with olive oil on both sides.
2. Season with sea salt, black pepper, and chopped rosemary, ensuring the chop is evenly coated.
3. Place the seasoned lamb T-bone chop on the preheated grill.
4. Grill for 4-5 minutes on each side for medium-rare, or longer depending on your preferred level of doneness. Use a meat thermometer to ensure the internal temperature reaches 145°F for medium-rare. Once cooked to your liking, remove the lamb T-bone from the grill and let it rest for 5 minutes to allow the juices to redistribute.

Nutritional Values: Calories: 420 kcal; **Protein:** 30g; **Fat:** 34g; **Carbohydrates:** 0g; **Sodium:** 600mg

GARLIC BUTTER LAMB CHOPS RECIPE

Preparation Time: 5 minutes
Cooking Time: 10 minutes
Portions: 1 person
Ingredients:
- 2 lamb chops (approximately 6-8 oz total)
- 2 tbsp butter, softened
- 1 garlic clove, minced (or 1/2 tsp garlic powder)
- 1/2 tsp sea salt
- 1/4 tsp black pepper
- 1/2 tsp fresh rosemary, finely chopped

Instructions:
1. In a small bowl, combine the softened butter, minced garlic, and chopped rosemary. Mix until well blended. Pat the lamb chops dry with paper towels to ensure a good sear. Season both sides of the lamb chops with sea salt and black pepper.
2. Heat a skillet over medium-high heat. Add the seasoned lamb chops to the skillet and sear for 3-4 minutes on the first side without moving them, to develop a nice crust. Flip the lamb chops and cook for an additional 3-4 minutes on the other side, or until they reach your desired level of doneness.
3. In the last minute of cooking, add the garlic butter mixture to the skillet. Use a spoon to baste the lamb chops with the melted garlic butter as they finish cooking.
4. Once cooked, remove the lamb chops from the skillet and let them rest for a few minutes to allow the juices to redistribute. Serve the lamb chops with the garlic butter drizzled over the top.

Nutritional Values: Calories: 450 kcal; **Protein:** 25g; **Fat:** 38g; **Carbohydrates:** 0g; **Sodium:** 600mg

GRILLED LAMB SKEWERS RECIPE

Preparation Time: 10 minutes
Cooking Time: 10-12 minutes
Portions: 1 person
Ingredients:
- 8 oz lamb shoulder, cut into 1-inch cubes
- 1 tbsp olive oil
- 1/2 tsp sea salt
- 1/4 tsp black pepper
- 1/2 tsp dried thyme (or fresh thyme, chopped)
- Skewers (metal or soaked wooden skewers)

Instructions:
1. In a bowl, combine the lamb cubes with olive oil, sea salt, black pepper, and thyme. Toss the lamb to ensure all pieces are evenly coated with the seasoning and oil. Thread the seasoned lamb cubes onto the skewers, leaving a little space between each piece for even cooking.
2. Preheat your grill to medium-high heat. Ensure the grill grates are clean and lightly oiled to prevent sticking.
3. Place the skewers on the preheated grill. Cook for about 4-5 minutes on each side, turning occasionally to ensure even cooking and a nice char on all sides. Grill until the lamb is cooked to your desired level of doneness (internal temperature of 145°F/63°C for medium-rare).
4. Once cooked, remove the skewers from the grill and let them rest for a few minutes.

Nutritional Values: Calories: 400 kcal; **Protein:** 30g; **Fat:** 30g; **Carbohydrates:** 0g; **Sodium:** 600mg

HOMEMADE LAMB SAUSAGES RECIPE

Preparation Time: 10 minutes
Cooking Time: 10 minutes
Portions: 1 person
Ingredients:
- 6 oz ground lamb
- 1/2 tsp sea salt
- 1/4 tsp black pepper
- 1/4 tsp dried thyme
- 1/4 tsp garlic powder
- 1 tbsp ghee (for cooking)

Instructions:
1. In a bowl, mix ground lamb with sea salt, black pepper, thyme, and garlic powder. Form the seasoned lamb mixture into small sausage patties.
2. Heat ghee in a skillet over medium heat.
3. Cook the sausage patties for 4-5 minutes on each side until browned and cooked through.
4. Remove from the skillet and let rest for a minute. Serve the sausages hot.

Nutritional Values: Calories: 350 kcal; **Protein:** 25g; **Fat** 28g; **Carbohydrates** 0g; **Sodium** 500mg

LAMB AND EGG SCRAMBLE

Preparation Time: 5 minutes
Cooking Time: 10 minutes
Portions: 1 person
Ingredients:
- 4 oz ground lamb
- 2 large eggs
- 1 tbsp butter
- 1/2 tsp sea salt
- 1/4 tsp black pepper
- 1 tsp ghee

Instructions:
1. In a skillet, melt the ghee over medium heat. Add the ground lamb to the skillet, season with sea salt and black pepper, and cook for 5-7 minutes until browned and cooked through. Remove the lamb from the skillet and set aside.
2. In the same skillet, add the butter and let it melt over medium heat.
3. Crack the eggs into the skillet and scramble them, stirring gently until they are just set.
4. Return the cooked lamb to the skillet with the eggs.
5. Stir everything together until the lamb and eggs are well combined and heated through.
6. Taste the scramble and adjust seasoning with additional salt and pepper if needed.
7. Serve the lamb and egg scramble hot, straight from the skillet.

Nutritional Values: Calories: 450 kcal; **Protein:** 30g; **Fat:** 38g; **Carbohydrates:** 0g; **Sodium:** 600mg

LAMB MEATBALLS RECIPE

Preparation Time: 10 minutes
Cooking Time: 15 minutes
Portions: 1 person
Ingredients:
- 6 oz ground lamb
- 1/2 tsp sea salt
- 1/4 tsp black pepper
- 1/4 tsp garlic powder
- 1/4 tsp dried thyme
- 1 tbsp ghee (for cooking)

Instructions:
1. In a bowl, combine the ground lamb with sea salt, black pepper, garlic powder, and dried thyme. Mix well until all ingredients are evenly distributed.
2. Shape the seasoned lamb mixture into small meatballs, about 1 inch in diameter. You should get around 6-8 meatballs. In a skillet, melt the ghee over medium heat.
3. Add the meatballs to the skillet and cook for about 7-8 minutes, turning occasionally to ensure they brown evenly on all sides. The meatballs should be cooked through and reach an internal temperature of 160°F.
4. Once cooked, remove the meatballs from the skillet and let them rest for a minute.
5. Serve the lamb meatballs hot, either on their own or with a carnivore-friendly sauce.

Nutritional Values: Calories: 350 kcal; **Protein:** 25g; **Fat:** 28g; **Carbohydrates:** 0g; **Sodium:** 600mg

LAMB WITH THYME AND LEMON RECIPE

Preparation Time: 10 minutes
Cooking Time: 30-35 minutes
Portions: 1 person
Ingredients:
- 7 oz lamb shoulder, cut into chunks
- 1 tsp fresh thyme (or 1/2 tsp dried thyme)
- 1 lemon wedge (optional)
- 1/2 tsp sea salt
- 1/4 tsp black pepper
- 1 tbsp butter

Instructions:
1. Preheat your oven to 375°F. Season the lamb shoulder chunks with sea salt, black pepper, and thyme. In an oven-safe skillet, melt the butter over medium-high heat. Sear the lamb chunks for 2-3 minutes on each side until browned.
2. Transfer the skillet with the seared lamb to the preheated oven. Roast for 25-30 minutes until the lamb is tender and cooked to your desired level of doneness.
3. If desired, squeeze a lemon wedge over the lamb before serving to add a touch of acidity.
4. Serve the lamb hot, drizzled with any pan juices from the skillet.

Nutritional Values: Calories: 420 kcal; **Protein:** 31g; **Fat:** 34g; **Carbohydrates:** 0g; **Sodium:** 620mg.

MINTED LAMB STEW RECIPE

Preparation Time: 10 minutes
Cooking Time: 1 hour
Portions: 1 person
Ingredients:
- 8 oz lamb cubes
- 1 tbsp fresh mint, chopped
- 1 tbsp butter
- 1/2 tsp sea salt
- 1/4 tsp black pepper

Instructions:
1. Season the lamb cubes with sea salt and black pepper.
2. In a medium pot, melt the butter over medium-high heat. Add the lamb cubes and sear on all sides until browned, about 5-7 minutes.
3. Stir in the chopped fresh mint and mix well with the lamb. Reduce the heat to low, cover the pot, and let the lamb simmer for about 45 minutes to 1 hour, until the meat is tender. Stir occasionally.
4. Taste the stew and adjust seasoning if necessary, adding more salt and pepper to taste. Serve the minted lamb stew hot, garnished with extra fresh mint if desired.

Nutritional Values: Calories: 400 kcal; **Protein:** 30g; **Fat:** 30g; **Carbohydrates:** 0g; **Sodium:** 700mg

ROASTED LAMB WITH ROSEMARY RECIPE

Preparation Time: 10 minutes
Cooking Time: 1 hour
Portions: 1 person
Ingredients:
- 8 oz lamb leg
- 1 clove garlic, minced
- 1 tsp fresh rosemary, chopped (or 1/2 tsp dried rosemary)
- 1/2 tsp sea salt
- 1/4 tsp black pepper
- 1 tbsp butter

Instructions:
1. Preheat your oven to 375°F. In a small bowl, mix the minced garlic, chopped rosemary, sea salt, and black pepper.
2. Rub the lamb leg with the garlic and rosemary mixture, ensuring it's evenly coated.
3. In an oven-safe skillet, melt the butter over medium-high heat.
4. Sear the lamb leg on all sides until browned, about 3-4 minutes per side.
5. Transfer the skillet with the seared lamb leg to the preheated oven. Roast for 45 minutes to 1 hour, or until the internal temperature reaches your desired level of doneness (145°F for medium-rare).
6. Once cooked, remove the lamb from the oven and let it rest for 10 minutes to allow the juices to redistribute.
7. Slice the lamb leg and serve hot, drizzled with any pan juices.

Nutritional Values: Calories: 450 kcal; **Protein:** 35g; **Fat:** 34g; **Carbohydrates:** 0g; **Sodium:** 600mg

CHAPTER 7: POULTRY RECIPES

CHICKEN RECIPES

BACON-WRAPPED CHICKEN BREASTS RECIPE

Preparation Time: 10 minutes
Cooking Time: 25-30 minutes
Portions: 1 person
Ingredients:
- 1 boneless, skinless chicken breast (about 6 oz)
- 2 slices bacon
- 1/2 tsp sea salt
- 1/4 tsp black pepper
- 1/4 tsp garlic powder

Instructions:
1. Preheat your oven to 375°F. Season the chicken breast with sea salt, black pepper, and garlic powder on all sides. Wrap the seasoned chicken breast with the bacon slices, ensuring the ends of the bacon overlap slightly to stay in place. You can secure the bacon with toothpicks if necessary.
2. Place the bacon-wrapped chicken breast on a baking sheet or in an oven-safe skillet. Bake in the preheated oven for 25-30 minutes, or until the internal temperature of the chicken reaches 165°F and the bacon is crispy. Remove the chicken from the oven and let it rest for a few minutes before slicing. Serve the bacon-wrapped chicken breast hot, optionally garnished with more black pepper.

Nutritional Values: Calories: 350 kcal; **Protein:** 35g; **Fat:** 22g; **Carbohydrates:** 0g; **Sodium:** 700mg

BAKED CHICKEN DRUMSTICKS RECIPE

Preparation Time: 5 minutes
Cooking Time: 35-40 minutes
Portions: 1 person
Ingredients:
- 2 chicken drumsticks
- 1 tbsp butter, melted
- 1/2 tsp sea salt
- 1/4 tsp black pepper
- 1/4 tsp dried thyme

Instructions:
1. Preheat your oven to 400°F. In a small bowl, mix the melted butter, sea salt, black pepper, and dried thyme. Brush the chicken drumsticks with the seasoned butter mixture, making sure they are evenly coated. Place the drumsticks on a baking sheet lined with parchment paper or in an oven-safe dish. Bake for 35-40 minutes, turning halfway through, until the drumsticks are golden brown and have an internal temperature of 165°F.
2. Remove the drumsticks from the oven and let them rest for 5 minutes before serving.
3. Serve the baked chicken drumsticks hot, optionally garnished with a sprinkle of extra thyme.

Nutritional Values: Calories: 320 kcal; **Protein:** 25g; **Fat:** 24g; **Carbohydrates:** 0g; **Sodium:** 450mg

CHICKEN AND BACON SKEWERS RECIPE

Preparation Time: 10 minutes
Cooking Time: 15-20 minutes
Portions: 1 person
Ingredients:

- 4 oz chicken breast, cut into bite-sized cubes
- 2 slices bacon, cut into thirds
- 1/2 tsp sea salt
- 1/4 tsp black pepper
- 1 tsp olive oil

Instructions:

1. Preheat your grill to medium-high heat. Season the chicken cubes with sea salt and black pepper. Alternate threading the chicken cubes and bacon pieces onto the skewers.
2. Lightly brush the assembled skewers with olive oil to help prevent sticking and enhance browning. Place the skewers on the preheated grill.
3. Grill for 15-20 minutes, turning occasionally, until the chicken is cooked through, and the bacon is crispy. The chicken should reach an internal temperature of 165°F.
4. Once cooked, remove the skewers from the grill and let them rest for a couple of minutes. Serve the chicken and bacon skewers hot, optionally with a sprinkle of additional black pepper.

Nutritional Values: Calories: 320 kcal; **Protein:** 28g; **Fat:** 22g; **Carbohydrates:** 0g; **Sodium:** 650mg

CHICKEN BREAST WITH LEMON BUTTER RECIPE

Preparation Time: 5 minutes
Cooking Time: 15-20 minutes
Portions: 1 person
Ingredients:

- 1 boneless, skinless chicken breast (about 6 oz)
- 2 tbsp butter
- 1 tsp lemon juice (optional)
- 1/2 tsp sea salt
- 1/4 tsp black pepper

Instructions:

1. Heat a skillet over medium heat and melt 1 tablespoon of butter. Season the chicken breast with sea salt and black pepper on both sides.
2. Place the chicken breast in the skillet and cook for 6-8 minutes on each side, or until the internal temperature reaches 165°F and the chicken is golden brown.
3. Reduce the heat to low. Add the remaining 1 tablespoon of butter to the skillet.
4. If using, add the lemon juice to the butter and stir until melted and combined, basting the chicken with the lemon butter sauce.
5. Remove the chicken breast from the skillet and let it rest for a few minutes to allow the juices to redistribute.
6. Serve the chicken breast hot, drizzled with the remaining lemon butter sauce from the skillet.

Nutritional Values: Calories: 300 kcal; **Protein:** 28g; **Fat:** 20g; **Carbohydrates:** 0g; **Sodium:** 500mg

CRISPY CHICKEN WINGS RECIPE

Preparation Time: 5 minutes
Cooking Time: 40-45 minutes
Portions: 1 person
Ingredients:
- 6 chicken wings
- 2 tbsp ghee, melted
- 1/2 tsp sea salt
- 1/4 tsp black pepper
- 1/4 tsp garlic powder

Instructions:
1. Preheat your oven to 400°F. In a large bowl, toss the chicken wings with melted ghee, sea salt, black pepper, and garlic powder until evenly coated.
2. Place the seasoned wings on a baking sheet lined with parchment paper or on a wire rack placed on a baking sheet to allow air circulation for extra crispiness.
3. Bake the wings in the preheated oven for 40-45 minutes, turning them halfway through, until they are golden brown and crispy.
4. Once cooked, remove the wings from the oven and let them rest for a few minutes.
5. Serve the crispy chicken wings hot, optionally garnished with extra sea salt or a sprinkle of black pepper.

Nutritional Values: Calories: 450 kcal; **Protein:** 28g; **Fat:** 36g; **Carbohydrates:** 0g; **Sodium:** 700mg

GRILLED CHICKEN DRUMSTICKS RECIPE

Preparation Time: 5 minutes
Cooking Time: 25-30 minutes
Portions: 1 person
Ingredients:
- 2 chicken drumsticks
- 1 tbsp olive oil
- 1/2 tsp sea salt
- 1/4 tsp black pepper
- 1/4 tsp paprika

Instructions:
1. Preheat your grill to medium-high heat. In a small bowl, mix the olive oil, sea salt, black pepper, and paprika.
2. Rub the mixture evenly over the chicken drumsticks, ensuring they are well coated. Place the drumsticks on the preheated grill.
3. Grill for 25-30 minutes, turning occasionally to ensure even cooking, until the internal temperature reaches 165°F and the drumsticks are cooked through and have a nice char.
4. Once cooked, remove the drumsticks from the grill and let them rest for a few minutes.
5. Serve the grilled chicken drumsticks hot, optionally garnished with an extra sprinkle of paprika.

Nutritional Values: Calories: 320 kcal; **Protein:** 26g; **Fat:** 22g; **Carbohydrates:** 0g; **Sodium:** 450mg

HERBED CHICKEN WINGS RECIPE

Preparation Time: 5 minutes
Cooking Time: 40-45 minutes
Portions: 1 person
Ingredients:
- 6 chicken wings
- 1 tbsp ghee, melted
- 1/2 tsp fresh rosemary, chopped (or 1/4 tsp dried rosemary)
- 1/2 tsp fresh thyme, chopped (or 1/4 tsp dried thyme)
- 1/2 tsp sea salt
- 1/4 tsp black pepper

Instructions:
1. Preheat your oven to 400°F. In a large bowl, toss the chicken wings with melted ghee, rosemary, thyme, sea salt, and black pepper until evenly coated.
2. Place the seasoned wings on a baking sheet lined with parchment paper or on a wire rack placed on a baking sheet to allow air circulation for extra crispiness.
3. Bake the wings in the preheated oven for 40-45 minutes, turning them halfway through, until they are golden brown and crispy.
4. Once cooked, remove the wings from the oven and let them rest for a few minutes.
5. Serve the herbed chicken wings hot, optionally garnished with extra rosemary or thyme.

Nutritional Values: Calories: 450 kcal; **Protein:** 28g; **Fat:** 36g; **Carbohydrates:** 0g; **Sodium:** 700mg

PAN-FRIED CHICKEN BREASTS RECIPE

Preparation Time: 5 minutes
Cooking Time: 12-15 minutes
Portions: 1 person
Ingredients:
- 1 boneless, skinless chicken breast (about 6 oz)
- 1 tbsp ghee
- 1/2 tsp sea salt
- 1/4 tsp black pepper
- 1/4 tsp garlic powder

Instructions:
1. Heat a skillet over medium heat and melt the ghee. Season the chicken breast with sea salt, black pepper, and garlic powder on both sides. Place the seasoned chicken breast in the hot skillet.
2. Cook for 6-7 minutes on each side, or until the internal temperature reaches 165°F and the chicken is golden brown.
3. While cooking, occasionally spoon some of the melted ghee over the chicken to keep it moist and flavorful.
4. Once cooked, remove the chicken breast from the skillet and let it rest for a few minutes to allow the juices to redistribute. Serve the pan-fried chicken breast hot, optionally garnished with a sprinkle of extra black pepper.

Nutritional Values: Calories: 300 kcal; **Protein:** 28g; **Fat:** 20g; **Carbohydrates:** 0g; **Sodium:** 450mg

ROASTED CHICKEN QUARTERS RECIPE

Preparation Time: 5 minutes
Cooking Time: 45-50 minutes
Portions: 1 person
Ingredients:
- 1 chicken quarter (about 10 oz)
- 1 tbsp olive oil
- 1/2 tsp sea salt
- 1/4 tsp black pepper
- 1/2 tsp dried thyme

Instructions:
1. Preheat your oven to 400°F. In a small bowl, mix the olive oil, sea salt, black pepper, and thyme. Rub the mixture all over the chicken quarter, ensuring it is evenly coated.
2. Place the seasoned chicken quarter on a baking sheet or in an oven-safe dish.
3. Roast the chicken quarter in the preheated oven for 45-50 minutes, or until the internal temperature reaches 165°F and the skin is golden brown and crispy.
4. Once cooked, remove the chicken from the oven and let it rest for 5 minutes to allow the juices to redistribute.
5. Serve the roasted chicken quarter hot, optionally garnished with an extra sprinkle of thyme.

Nutritional Values: Calories: 450 kcal; **Protein:** 30g; **Fat:** 34g; **Carbohydrates:** 0g; **Sodium:** 600mg

SPICY CHICKEN WINGS RECIPE

Preparation Time: 5 minutes
Cooking Time: 40-45 minutes
Portions: 1 person
Ingredients:
- 6 chicken wings
- 2 tbsp ghee, melted
- 1/2 tsp sea salt
- 1/4 tsp black pepper
- 1/4 tsp cayenne pepper

Instructions:
1. Preheat your oven to 400°F. In a large bowl, toss the chicken wings with melted ghee, sea salt, black pepper, and cayenne pepper until evenly coated.
2. Place the seasoned wings on a baking sheet lined with parchment paper or on a wire rack placed on a baking sheet to allow air circulation for extra crispiness.
3. Bake the wings in the preheated oven for 40-45 minutes, turning them halfway through, until they are golden brown and crispy.
4. Once cooked, remove the wings from the oven and let them rest for a few minutes.
5. Serve the spicy chicken wings hot, optionally garnished with a sprinkle of extra cayenne pepper for added heat.

Nutritional Values: Calories: 450 kcal; **Protein:** 28g; **Fat:** 36g; **Carbohydrates:** 0g; **Sodium:** 700mg

TURKEY RECIPES

BUTTER-BASTED TURKEY THIGHS RECIPE

Preparation Time: 5 minutes
Cooking Time: 45-50 minutes
Portions: 1 person
Ingredients:
- 1 turkey thigh (about 8 oz)
- 2 tbsp butter, melted
- 1/2 tsp sea salt
- 1/4 tsp black pepper
- 1/2 tsp dried rosemary (or fresh if preferred)

Instructions:
1. Preheat your oven to 375°F.
2. Season the turkey thigh with sea salt, black pepper, and rosemary. Brush the thigh with melted butter, making sure it is evenly coated.
3. Place the turkey thigh on a baking sheet or in an oven-safe dish.
4. Roast the turkey thigh in the preheated oven for 45-50 minutes, occasionally basting with the melted butter. The turkey should reach an internal temperature of 165°F. Once cooked, remove the turkey thigh from the oven and let it rest for 5 minutes to allow the juices to redistribute.
5. Serve the butter-basted turkey thigh hot, optionally garnished with additional rosemary.

Nutritional Values: Calories: 400 kcal; **Protein:** 28g; **Fat:** 32g; **Carbohydrates:** 0g; **Sodium:** 600mg

GRILLED TURKEY BURGERS RECIPE

Preparation Time: 5 minutes
Cooking Time: 10-12 minutes
Portions: 1 person
Ingredients:
- 6 oz ground turkey
- 1/2 tsp sea salt
- 1/4 tsp black pepper
- 1/4 tsp garlic powder
- 1/2 tbsp ghee (for grilling)

Instructions:
1. Preheat your grill to medium-high heat.
2. In a bowl, mix the ground turkey with sea salt, black pepper, and garlic powder until well combined.
3. Form the seasoned turkey mixture into a patty.
4. Brush the grill grates with ghee to prevent sticking. Place the turkey patty on the grill and cook for 5-6 minutes on each side, or until the internal temperature reaches 165°F and the burger is cooked through.
5. Once cooked, remove the turkey burger from the grill and let it rest for a few minutes.
6. Serve the grilled turkey burger hot, optionally with a sprinkle of additional black pepper.

Nutritional Values: Calories: 250 kcal; **Protein:** 28g; **Fat:** 15g; **Carbohydrates:** 0g; **Sodium:** 400mg

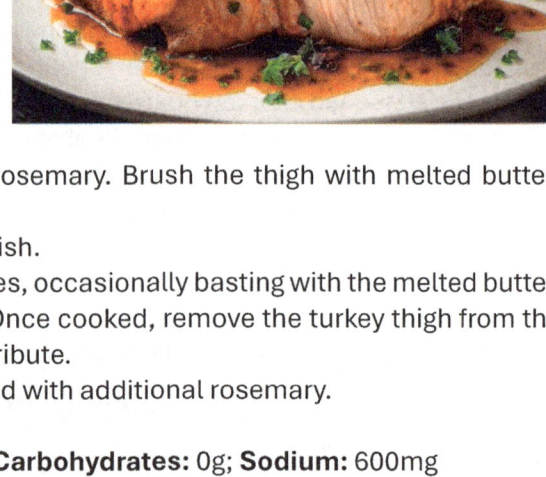

HERBED TURKEY CUTLETS RECIPE

Preparation Time: 5 minutes
Cooking Time: 10-12 minutes
Portions: 1 person
Ingredients:
- 1 turkey cutlet (about 6 oz)
- 1 tbsp butter
- 1/2 tsp dried thyme (or fresh if preferred)
- 1/2 tsp dried rosemary (or fresh if preferred)
- 1/2 tsp sea salt
- 1/4 tsp black pepper

Instructions:
1. Heat a skillet over medium heat and melt the butter.
2. Season the turkey cutlet with sea salt, black pepper, thyme, and rosemary on both sides. Place the seasoned turkey cutlet in the hot skillet. Cook for 4-6 minutes on each side, or until the internal temperature reaches 165°F and the cutlet is golden brown and cooked through.
3. While cooking, occasionally spoon some of the melted butter over the turkey cutlet to keep it moist and flavorful.
4. Once cooked, remove the turkey cutlet from the skillet and let it rest for a few minutes to allow the juices to redistribute.
5. Serve the herbed turkey cutlet hot, optionally garnished with a sprinkle of extra rosemary or thyme.

Nutritional Values: Calories: 280 kcal; **Protein:** 28g; **Fat:** 18g; **Carbohydrates:** 0g; **Sodium:** 500mg

PAN-FRIED TURKEY SAUSAGE PATTIES RECIPE

Preparation Time: 5 minutes
Cooking Time: 10-12 minutes
Portions: 1 person
Ingredients:
- 6 oz ground turkey
- 1/2 tsp sea salt
- 1/4 tsp black pepper
- 1/4 tsp dried sage
- 1/4 tsp garlic powder
- 1 tbsp ghee (for frying)

Instructions:
1. In a bowl, combine the ground turkey, sea salt, black pepper, sage, and garlic powder. Mix well until the seasonings are evenly distributed.
2. Divide the seasoned turkey mixture into 2-3 equal portions and shape them into small patties.
3. Heat a skillet over medium heat and add the ghee. Place the turkey patties in the hot skillet.
4. Cook for 4-6 minutes on each side, or until the patties are golden brown and the internal temperature reaches 165°F.
5. Once cooked, remove the patties from the skillet and let them rest for a few minutes.
6. Serve the turkey sausage patties hot, optionally garnished with a sprinkle of extra black pepper.

Nutritional Values: Calories: 220 kcal; **Protein:** 22g; **Fat:** 14g; **Carbohydrates:** 0g; **Sodium:** 450mg

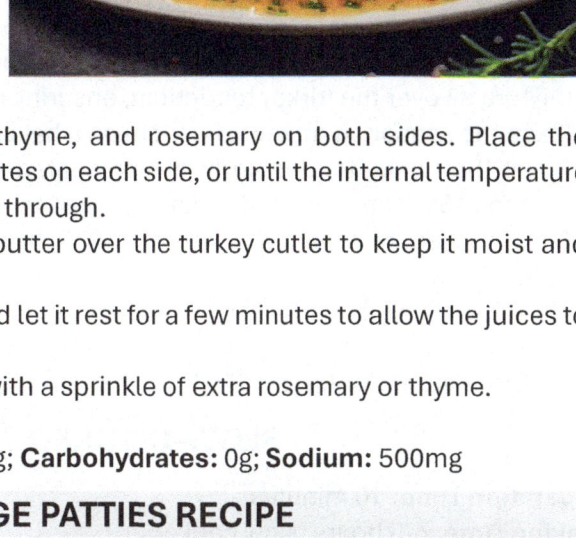

ROASTED TURKEY TENDERLOINS RECIPE

Preparation Time: 5 minutes
Cooking Time: 25-30 minutes
Portions: 1 person
Ingredients:
- 1 turkey tenderloin (about 6-8 oz)
- 1 tbsp olive oil
- 1/2 tsp sea salt
- 1/4 tsp black pepper
- 1/2 tsp dried thyme (or fresh if preferred)

Instructions:
1. Preheat your oven to 375°F. In a small bowl, mix the olive oil, sea salt, black pepper, and thyme. Rub the mixture all over the turkey tenderloin, ensuring it is evenly coated.
2. Place the seasoned turkey tenderloin on a baking sheet or in an oven-safe dish.
3. Roast the turkey tenderloin in the preheated oven for 25-30 minutes, or until the internal temperature reaches 165°F and the tenderloin is cooked through and golden brown.
4. Once cooked, remove the turkey tenderloin from the oven and let it rest for 5 minutes to allow the juices to redistribute.
5. Slice the turkey tenderloin and serve hot, optionally garnished with a sprinkle of extra thyme.

Nutritional Values: Calories: 250 kcal; **Protein:** 30g; **Fat:** 12g; **Carbohydrates:** 0g; **Sodium:** 450mg

SLOW-COOKED TURKEY BREAST RECIPE

Preparation Time: 10 minutes
Cooking Time: 4-5 hours (slow cooker)
Portions: 1 person
Ingredients:
- 1 turkey breast (about 8 oz)
- 2 tbsp butter, melted
- 1/2 tsp sea salt
- 1/4 tsp black pepper
- 1/2 tsp dried thyme (or fresh if preferred)

Instructions:
1. Season the turkey breast with sea salt, black pepper, and thyme.
2. Brush the turkey breast with the melted butter, ensuring it is evenly coated.
3. Set your slow cooker to the low setting.
4. Place the seasoned and buttered turkey breast into the slow cooker. Cover and cook on low for 4-5 hours, or until the internal temperature reaches 165°F and the turkey is tender. If possible, baste the turkey breast with the juices in the slow cooker once or twice during the cooking process to keep it moist.
5. Once cooked, remove the turkey breast from the slow cooker and let it rest for 5 minutes to allow the juices to redistribute.
6. Slice the turkey breast and serve hot, optionally garnished with a sprinkle of additional thyme.

Nutritional Values: Calories: 320 kcal; **Protein:** 30g; **Fat:** 20g; **Carbohydrates:** 0g; **Sodium:** 500mg

SPICY TURKEY MEATBALLS RECIPE

Preparation Time: 10 minutes
Cooking Time: 15-20 minutes
Portions: 1 person
Ingredients:
- 6 oz ground turkey
- 1/2 tsp sea salt
- 1/4 tsp black pepper
- 1/4 tsp garlic powder
- 1/4 tsp cayenne pepper
- 1 tbsp ghee (for cooking)

Instructions:
1. In a bowl, combine the ground turkey, sea salt, black pepper, garlic powder, and cayenne pepper. Mix until the seasonings are evenly distributed.
2. Shape the seasoned turkey mixture into small meatballs, about 1 inch in diameter. You should get around 6-8 meatballs. Heat a skillet over medium heat and add the ghee. Place the meatballs in the hot skillet and cook for 7-10 minutes, turning occasionally to ensure they are browned on all sides and cooked through. The internal temperature should reach 165°F.
3. Once cooked, remove the meatballs from the skillet and let them rest for a few minutes.
4. Serve the spicy turkey meatballs hot, optionally garnished with an extra sprinkle of cayenne pepper for added heat.

Nutritional Values: Calories: 230 kcal; **Protein:** 26g; **Fat:** 14g; **Carbohydrates:** 0g; **Sodium:** 500mg

TURKEY BREAST WITH LEMON BUTTER RECIPE

Preparation Time: 5 minutes
Cooking Time: 15-20 minutes
Portions: 1 person
Ingredients:
- 1 turkey breast (about 6-8 oz)
- 2 tbsp butter
- 1 tsp lemon juice (optional)
- 1/2 tsp sea salt
- 1/4 tsp black pepper

Instructions:
1. Heat a skillet over medium heat and melt 1 tablespoon of butter.
2. Season the turkey breast with sea salt and black pepper on both sides.
3. Place the seasoned turkey breast in the skillet and cook for 6-8 minutes on each side, or until the internal temperature reaches 165°F and the turkey is golden brown.
4. Reduce the heat to low. Add the remaining 1 tablespoon of butter to the skillet.
5. If using, add the lemon juice to the butter and stir until melted and combined, basting the turkey breast with the lemon butter sauce.
6. Once cooked, remove the turkey breast from the skillet and let it rest for a few minutes to allow the juices to redistribute.
7. Serve the turkey breast hot, drizzled with the remaining lemon butter sauce from the skillet.

Nutritional Values: Calories: 320 kcal; **Protein:** 28g; **Fat:** 22g; **Carbohydrates:** 0g; **Sodium:** 500mg

TURKEY THIGHS WITH SAGE BUTTER RECIPE

Preparation Time: 5 minutes
Cooking Time: 40-45 minutes
Portions: 1 person
Ingredients:
- 1 turkey thigh (about 8 oz)
- 2 tbsp butter, softened
- 1/2 tsp dried sage (or 1 tsp fresh sage, finely chopped)
- 1/2 tsp sea salt
- 1/4 tsp black pepper

Instructions:
1. Preheat your oven to 375°F. In a small bowl, mix the softened butter with the sage, sea salt, and black pepper until well combined.
2. Rub the sage butter mixture all over the turkey thigh, making sure it is evenly coated.
3. Place the seasoned turkey thigh on a baking sheet or in an oven-safe dish. Roast in the preheated oven for 40-45 minutes, or until the internal temperature reaches 165°F and the skin is golden brown and crispy.
4. Once cooked, remove the turkey thigh from the oven and let it rest for 5 minutes to allow the juices to redistribute.
5. Serve the turkey thigh hot, optionally garnished with additional fresh sage.

Nutritional Values: Calories: 400 kcal; **Protein:** 28g; **Fat:** 32g; **Carbohydrates:** 0g; **Sodium:** 550mg

SMOKED TURKEY THIGHS RECIPE

Preparation Time: 10 minutes (plus 1 hour for pre-smoking preparation)
Cooking Time: 2-3 hours
Portions: 1 person
Ingredients:
- 1 turkey thigh (about 8 oz)
- 1 tbsp olive oil
- 1/2 tsp sea salt
- 1/4 tsp black pepper
- 1/4 tsp garlic powder
- 1/4 tsp smoked paprika

Instructions:
1. Rub the turkey thigh with olive oil, sea salt, black pepper, garlic powder, and smoked paprika.
2. Let the turkey thigh sit at room temperature for about 1 hour to allow the flavors to penetrate.
3. Preheat your smoker to 225°F. If you don't have a smoker, you can use a grill set up for indirect cooking with wood chips for smoke. Place the seasoned turkey thigh in the smoker.
4. Smoke the turkey thigh for 2-3 hours, or until the internal temperature reaches 165°F. The exact time will depend on the size of the thigh and the consistency of your smoker's temperature. If desired, baste the turkey thigh with its own juices or a bit of additional olive oil every 30 minutes to keep it moist.
5. Once the turkey thigh reaches the desired temperature, remove it from the smoker and let it rest for 10 minutes.
6. Serve the smoked turkey thigh hot, optionally garnished with a sprinkle of additional smoked paprika for extra flavor.

Nutritional Values: Calories: 380 kcal; **Protein:** 28g; **Fat:** 28g; **Carbohydrates:** 0g; **Sodium:** 600mg

DUCK RECIPES

CAJUN-SPICED DUCK BREAST RECIPE

Preparation Time: 5 minutes
Cooking Time: 15-20 minutes
Portions: 1 person
Ingredients:
- 1 duck breast (about 6 oz)
- 1 tbsp ghee
- 1/2 tsp sea salt
- 1/4 tsp black pepper
- 1/2 tsp Cajun seasoning

Instructions:
1. Heat a skillet over medium heat and add the ghee. Season the duck breast with sea salt, black pepper, and Cajun seasoning on both sides. Using a sharp knife, gently score the skin of the duck breast in a crosshatch pattern. This will help the fat render and create a crispy skin.
2. Place the duck breast skin-side down in the hot skillet. Cook for 6-8 minutes until the skin is crispy and golden brown, then flip and cook for an additional 4-6 minutes until the internal temperature reaches 135°F for medium-rare or 145°F for medium.
3. Remove the duck breast from the skillet and let it rest for 5 minutes to allow the juices to redistribute. Slice the duck breast and serve hot, optionally garnished with an extra sprinkle of Cajun seasoning.

Nutritional Values: Calories: 400 kcal; **Protein:** 25g; **Fat:** 32g; **Carbohydrates:** 0g; **Sodium:** 550mg

CRISPY DUCK SKIN CHIPS RECIPE

Preparation Time: 5 minutes
Cooking Time: 10-15 minutes
Portions: 1 person
Ingredients:
- Duck skin (from 1 duck breast)
- 1/4 tsp sea salt
- 1/4 tsp black pepper
- 1 tbsp duck fat (optional, for extra crispiness)

Instructions:
1. Preheat your oven to 400°F. Lay the duck skin flat on a cutting board.
2. Season with sea salt and black pepper on both sides. If desired, heat a skillet over medium heat and add the duck skin. Cook for 2-3 minutes on each side to render some fat, which will help the skin crisp up even more. Alternatively, you can use the duck fat.
3. Place the seasoned duck skin on a baking sheet lined with parchment paper. Bake in the preheated oven for 10-15 minutes, or until the skin is golden brown and crispy. Remove the duck skin from the oven and transfer to a paper towel-lined plate to cool and drain any excess fat. Serve the crispy duck skin chips as a snack or garnish.

Nutritional Values: Calories: 150 kcal; **Protein:** 6g; **Fat:** 14g; **Carbohydrates:** 0g; **Sodium:** 300mg

DUCK BREAST WITH BLACK PEPPER BUTTER RECIPE

Preparation Time: 5 minutes
Cooking Time: 15-20 minutes
Portions: 1 person
Ingredients:
- 1 duck breast (about 6 oz)
- 2 tbsp butter
- 1 tsp freshly ground black pepper
- 1/2 tsp sea salt
- 1/2 tsp garlic powder

Instructions:
1. Preheat your oven to 400°F. Pat the duck breast dry with paper towels. Season both sides with sea salt and garlic powder. Using a sharp knife, gently score the skin of the duck breast in a crosshatch pattern to help render the fat and create a crispy skin.
2. Heat a skillet over medium heat. Place the duck breast skin-side down in the hot skillet. Sear for 5-7 minutes until the skin is crispy and golden brown. Flip the duck breast and sear the other side for 2-3 minutes. In the skillet, add the butter and freshly ground black pepper. Allow the butter to melt and infuse with the pepper while basting the duck breast with the melted butter.
3. Transfer the skillet to the preheated oven and roast for 10-12 minutes, or until the internal temperature reaches 135°F for medium-rare or 145°F for medium. Remove the duck breast from the oven and let it rest for 5 minutes to allow the juices to redistribute. Slice the duck breast and serve hot, drizzled with the remaining black pepper butter from the skillet.

Nutritional Values: Calories: 470 kcal; **Protein:** 26g; **Fat:** 40g; **Carbohydrates:** 0g; **Sodium:** 580mg

DUCK BREAST WITH ROSEMARY BUTTER RECIPE

Preparation Time: 5 minutes
Cooking Time: 15-20 minutes
Portions: 1 person
Ingredients:
- 1 duck breast (about 6 oz)
- 2 tbsp butter
- 1/2 tsp fresh rosemary, finely chopped (or 1/4 tsp rosemary)
- 1/2 tsp sea salt
- 1/4 tsp black pepper

Instructions:
1. Heat a skillet over medium heat. Season the duck breast with sea salt and black pepper on both sides. Using a sharp knife, gently score the skin of the duck breast in a crosshatch pattern to help the fat render and create a crispy skin. Place the duck breast skin-side down in the hot skillet. Cook for 6-8 minutes until the skin is crispy and golden brown, then flip and cook for an additional 4-6 minutes until the internal temperature reaches 135°F for medium-rare or 145°F for medium.
2. While the duck is cooking, melt the butter in a small saucepan over low heat. Stir in the chopped rosemary and let it infuse for a minute or two. Once the duck breast is cooked to your desired doneness, remove it from the skillet and let it rest for 5 minutes. While resting, spoon the rosemary butter over the duck breast to coat it in the fragrant, buttery sauce. Slice the duck breast and serve hot, drizzled with any remaining rosemary butter.

Nutritional Values: Calories: 450 kcal; **Protein:** 25g; **Fat:** 36g; **Carbohydrates:** 0g; **Sodium:** 600mg

DUCK CONFIT WITH GARLIC AND THYME RECIPE

Preparation Time: 10 minutes
Cooking Time: 2-3 hours
Portions: 1 person
Ingredients:
- 1 duck leg (about 8 oz)
- 1 cup duck fat (enough to fully submerge the duck leg)
- 2 garlic cloves, crushed
- 1/2 tsp fresh thyme leaves (or 1/4 tsp dried thyme)
- 1/2 tsp sea salt
- 1/4 tsp black pepper

Instructions:
1. Season the duck leg with sea salt, black pepper, crushed garlic, and thyme. Rub the seasonings into the skin and meat. Let the seasoned duck leg sit at room temperature for about 30 minutes to allow the flavors to infuse. Preheat your oven to 225°F. Place the seasoned duck leg in an oven-safe dish. Pour the duck fat over the duck leg, ensuring it is fully submerged.
2. Cover the dish with foil and cook in the preheated oven for 2-3 hours, or until the duck meat is tender and easily pulls away from the bone. If you prefer a crispy skin, remove the duck leg from the duck fat and place it skin-side down in a hot skillet over medium-high heat. Cook for 2-3 minutes until the skin is crispy and golden brown.
3. Once cooked, let the duck leg rest for a few minutes. Serve the duck leg hot, optionally garnished with additional thyme.

Nutritional Values: Calories: 700 kcal; **Protein:** 28g; **Fat:** 65g; **Carbohydrates:** 0g; **Sodium:** 800mg

DUCK FAT ROASTED WHOLE DUCK WITH THYME RECIPE

Preparation Time: 15 minutes
Cooking Time: 2-2.5 hours
Portions: 1 person
Ingredients:
- 1 whole duck (about 4-5 lbs)
- 1/4 cup duck fat
- 1 tbsp fresh thyme leaves (or 1/2 tbsp dried thyme)
- 1 tsp sea salt
- 1/2 tsp black pepper
- 2 garlic cloves, crushed (optional)

Instructions:
1. Preheat your oven to 325°F. Pat the duck dry with paper towels. Rub the entire duck, inside and out, with duck fat. Season the duck generously with sea salt, black pepper, and thyme. If using, place the crushed garlic cloves inside the cavity of the duck.
2. Using a sharp knife, gently score the skin of the duck in a crosshatch pattern. This will help the fat render out during cooking, resulting in crispy skin. Place the duck breast-side up on a rack in a roasting pan. Roast in the preheated oven for 2-2.5 hours, or until the internal temperature reaches 165°F and the skin is golden brown and crispy. Baste the duck with its own rendered fat every 30 minutes for added flavor and moisture.
3. Once cooked, remove the duck from the oven and let it rest for 15 minutes to allow the juices to redistribute. Carve the duck and serve hot, optionally garnished with additional thyme.

Nutritional Values: Calories: 980 kcal; **Protein:** 56g; **Fat:** 80g; **Carbohydrates:** 0g; **Sodium:** 1200mg

DUCK THIGHS WITH GARLIC BUTTER AND THYME RECIPE

Preparation Time: 10 minutes
Cooking Time: 45-50 minutes
Portions: 1 person
Ingredients:
- 2 duck thighs (about 8 oz each)
- 2 tbsp butter
- 2 garlic cloves, minced
- 1 tsp fresh thyme leaves (or 1/2 tsp dried thyme)
- 1/2 tsp sea salt
- 1/4 tsp black pepper

Instructions:
1. Preheat your oven to 375°F. In a small saucepan, melt the butter over low heat. Add the minced garlic and thyme to the melted butter, stirring for about 1 minute until fragrant. Remove from heat. Pat the duck thighs dry with paper towels. Season both sides of the thighs with sea salt and black pepper.
2. Heat an oven-safe skillet over medium heat. Place the duck thighs skin-side down in the hot skillet and sear for 6-8 minutes, until the skin is crispy and golden brown.
3. Flip the duck thighs over in the skillet, then pour the garlic butter mixture over them. Transfer the skillet to the preheated oven and roast for 35-40 minutes, or until the internal temperature of the duck thighs reaches 165°F and the meat is tender.
4. Remove the duck thighs from the oven and let them rest for a few minutes. Serve hot, drizzled with any remaining garlic butter from the skillet.

Nutritional Values: Calories: 550 kcal; **Protein:** 38g; **Fat:** 44g; **Carbohydrates:** 0g; **Sodium:** 600mg

GARLIC HERB DUCK WINGS RECIPE

Preparation Time: 5 minutes
Cooking Time: 45-50 minutes
Portions: 1 person
Ingredients:
- 4 duck wings (about 1 lb)
- 2 tbsp ghee or duck fat
- 2 garlic cloves, minced
- 1 tsp fresh rosemary, finely chopped (or 1/2 tsp rosemary)
- 1/2 tsp sea salt
- 1/4 tsp black pepper

Instructions:
1. Preheat your oven to 375°F. In a small saucepan, melt the ghee or duck fat over low heat. Add the minced garlic and rosemary to the melted ghee, stirring for about 1 minute until fragrant.
2. Remove from heat. Pat the duck wings dry with paper towels. Season the wings on both sides with sea salt and black pepper.
3. Toss the duck wings in the garlic herb mixture until they are evenly coated.
4. Place the coated duck wings on a baking sheet lined with parchment paper. Roast in the preheated oven for 45-50 minutes, turning halfway through, until the wings are crispy and golden brown. Remove the duck wings from the oven and let them rest for a few minutes. Serve hot, optionally garnished with additional rosemary.

Nutritional Values: Calories: 650 kcal; **Protein:** 34g; **Fat:** 54g; **Carbohydrates:** 0g; **Sodium:** 720mg

ROASTED DUCK BREAST WITH SAGE RECIPE

Preparation Time: 5 minutes
Cooking Time: 20-25 minutes
Portions: 1 person
Ingredients:
- 1 duck breast (about 6 oz)
- 2 tbsp butter
- 1 tsp fresh sage, finely chopped (or 1/2 tsp dried sage)
- 1/2 tsp sea salt
- 1/4 tsp black pepper

Instructions:
1. Preheat your oven to 400°F. Pat the duck breast dry with paper towels. Season both sides with sea salt and black pepper. Using a sharp knife, gently score the skin of the duck breast in a crosshatch pattern, being careful not to cut into the meat.
2. Heat a skillet over medium heat. Place the duck breast skin-side down in the hot skillet. Sear for 5-7 minutes until the skin is crispy and golden brown. Flip the duck breast and sear the other side for 2-3 minutes. In the skillet, add the butter and chopped sage, allowing the butter to melt and infuse with the sage. Spoon some of the melted sage butter over the duck breast. Transfer the skillet to the preheated oven and roast for 10-15 minutes, or until the internal temperature reaches 135°F for medium-rare or 145°F for medium.
3. Remove the duck breast from the oven and let it rest for 5 minutes to allow the juices to redistribute. Slice the duck breast and serve hot, drizzled with the remaining sage butter from the skillet.

Nutritional Values: Calories: 480 kcal; **Protein:** 25g; **Fat:** 40g; **Carbohydrates:** 0g; **Sodium:** 600mg

SPICY DUCK DRUMSTICKS WITH SAGE RECIPE

Preparation Time: 10 minutes
Cooking Time: 45-50 minutes
Portions: 1 person
Ingredients:
- 2 duck drumsticks (about 8 oz each)
- 2 tbsp ghee or duck fat
- 1/2 tsp cayenne pepper
- 1 tsp fresh sage, finely chopped (or 1/2 tsp dried sage)
- 1/2 tsp sea salt
- 1/4 tsp black pepper

Instructions:
1. Preheat your oven to 375°F. In a small bowl, mix the cayenne pepper, sea salt, black pepper, and sage. Rub the duck drumsticks with the spice mixture, ensuring they are evenly coated.
2. Heat a skillet over medium heat and add the ghee or duck fat. Once the fat is melted and hot, sear the duck drumsticks on all sides until they are golden brown, about 5-7 minutes.
3. Transfer the seared drumsticks to an oven-safe dish or leave them in the skillet if it is oven-safe. Roast in the preheated oven for 35-40 minutes, or until the internal temperature reaches 165°F and the drumsticks are cooked through and crispy. Remove the duck drumsticks from the oven and let them rest for 5 minutes. Serve the spicy duck drumsticks hot, optionally garnished with additional fresh sage.

Nutritional Values: Calories: 510 kcal; **Protein:** 32g; **Fat:** 42g; **Carbohydrates:** 0g; **Sodium:** 680mg

CHAPTER 8: FISH AND SEAFOOD RECIPES

FISH RECIPES

BAKED COD WITH LEMON BUTTER RECIPE

Preparation Time: 5 minutes
Cooking Time: 15-20 minutes
Portions: 1 person
Ingredients:
- 1 cod fillet (about 6 oz)
- 2 tbsp butter
- 1 tsp lemon juice
- 1/2 tsp sea salt
- 1/4 tsp black pepper

Instructions:
1. Preheat your oven to 400°F. In a small saucepan, melt the butter over low heat. Add the lemon juice to the melted butter and stir well. Place the cod fillet in a small baking dish. Season both sides with sea salt and black pepper.
2. Pour the lemon butter mixture over the cod fillet, ensuring it is evenly coated.
3. Bake in the preheated oven for 15-20 minutes, or until the cod is opaque and flakes easily with a fork.
4. Remove the cod from the oven and serve hot, drizzled with any remaining lemon butter from the baking dish.

Nutritional Values: Calories: 290 kcal; **Protein:** 25g; **Fat:** 20g; **Carbohydrates:** 0g; **Sodium:** 520mg

BAKED SALMON WITH DILL RECIPE

Preparation Time: 5 minutes
Cooking Time: 15-20 minutes
Portions: 1 person
Ingredients:
- 1 salmon fillet (about 6 oz)
- 2 tbsp butter
- 1 tsp fresh dill, finely chopped (or 1/2 tsp dried dill)
- 1/2 tsp sea salt
- 1/4 tsp black pepper

Instructions:
1. Preheat your oven to 400°F.
2. In a small saucepan, melt the butter over low heat. Stir in the chopped dill until well combined.
3. Place the salmon fillet in a small baking dish. Season both sides with sea salt and black pepper. Pour the dill butter mixture over the salmon fillet, ensuring it is evenly coated.
4. Bake in the preheated oven for 15-20 minutes, or until the salmon is cooked through and flakes easily with a fork.
5. Remove the salmon from the oven and serve hot, drizzled with any remaining dill butter from the baking dish.

Nutritional Values: Calories: 350 kcal; **Protein:** 25g; **Fat:** 28g; **Carbohydrates:** 0g; **Sodium:** 540mg

ROASTED SEA BASS RECIPE

Preparation Time: 5 minutes
Cooking Time: 20-25 minutes
Portions: 1 person
Ingredients:
- 1 sea bass fillet (about 6 oz)
- 2 tbsp butter
- 1 tsp fresh thyme, finely chopped (or 1/2 tsp dried thyme)
- 1/2 tsp sea salt
- 1/4 tsp black pepper

Instructions:
1. Preheat your oven to 400°F.
2. In a small saucepan, melt the butter over low heat. Stir in the chopped thyme until well combined.
3. Place the sea bass fillet in a small baking dish. Season both sides with sea salt and black pepper.
4. Pour the thyme butter mixture over the sea bass fillet, ensuring it is evenly coated.
5. Roast in the preheated oven for 20-25 minutes, or until the sea bass is cooked through and flakes easily with a fork.
6. Remove the sea bass from the oven and serve hot, drizzled with any remaining thyme butter from the baking dish.

Nutritional Values: Calories: 320 kcal; **Protein:** 28g; **Fat:** 22g; **Carbohydrates:** 0g; **Sodium:** 560mg

SARDINES IN OLIVE OIL RECIPE

Preparation Time: 5 minutes
Cooking Time: 5 minutes
Portions: 1 person
Ingredients:
- 1 can of sardines in olive oil (about 3.75 oz)
- 1 tbsp extra virgin olive oil
- 1/2 tsp sea salt
- 1/4 tsp black pepper
- 1 tsp lemon juice (optional)
- 1 clove garlic, minced (optional)

Instructions:
1. Drain the sardines and place them on a plate.
2. In a small skillet, heat the extra virgin olive oil over medium heat. If using garlic, add the minced garlic to the skillet and sauté for about 1 minute, until fragrant.
3. Add the sardines to the skillet and cook for 2-3 minutes, gently turning them to warm through without breaking them apart.
4. Season the sardines with sea salt, black pepper, and optional lemon juice.
5. Serve the warm sardines immediately, drizzled with the remaining olive oil from the skillet.

Nutritional Values: Calories: 220 kcal; **Protein:** 22g; **Fat:** 15g; **Carbohydrates:** 0g; **Sodium:** 400mg

THYME-BASTED TROUT RECIPE

Preparation Time: 5 minutes
Cooking Time: 15-20 minutes
Portions: 1 person
Ingredients:
- 1 trout fillet (about 6 oz)
- 2 tbsp butter
- 1 tsp fresh thyme, finely chopped (or 1/2 tsp dried thyme)
- 1/2 tsp sea salt
- 1/4 tsp black pepper

Instructions:
1. Preheat your oven to 375°F. In a small saucepan, melt the butter over low heat. Stir in the chopped thyme until well combined.
2. Place the trout fillet in a small baking dish. Season both sides with sea salt and black pepper.
3. Pour half of the thyme butter mixture over the trout fillet, ensuring it is evenly coated.
4. Roast in the preheated oven for 15-20 minutes, or until the trout is cooked through and flakes easily with a fork. Halfway through the cooking time, baste the trout with the remaining thyme butter.
5. Remove the trout from the oven and serve hot, drizzled with any remaining thyme butter from the baking dish.

Nutritional Values: Calories: 320 kcal; **Protein:** 28g; **Fat:** 22g; **Carbohydrates:** 0g; **Sodium:** 450mg

SEAFOOD RECIPES

BUTTER-BASTED LOBSTER TAILS RECIPE

Preparation Time: 5 minutes
Cooking Time: 12-15 minutes
Portions: 1 person
Ingredients:
- 1 lobster tail (about 6 oz)
- 3 tbsp butter
- 1/2 tsp sea salt
- 1/4 tsp black pepper
- 1 tsp lemon juice (optional)
- 1 clove garlic, minced (optional)

Instructions:
1. Preheat your oven to 425°F. Using kitchen scissors, carefully cut down the top of the lobster shell to expose the meat. Gently lift the lobster meat above the shell while keeping it attached at the base, and place it on top of the shell.
2. In a small saucepan, melt the butter over low heat. If using, add the minced garlic and sauté for about 1 minute until fragrant. Stir in the lemon juice, sea salt, and black pepper. Place the lobster tail on a baking sheet. Generously brush the lobster meat with the butter mixture, reserving some for basting during cooking.
3. Roast the lobster tail in the preheated oven for 12-15 minutes, basting once halfway through, until the lobster meat is opaque and cooked through. Remove the lobster tail from the oven and serve hot, drizzled with the remaining butter mixture.

Nutritional Values: Calories: 320 kcal; **Protein:** 28g; **Fat:** 22g; **Carbohydrates:** 0g; **Sodium:** 380mg

CAJUN-SPICED SHRIMP RECIPE

Preparation Time: 5 minutes
Cooking Time: 5-7 minutes
Portions: 1 person
Ingredients:
- 6 large shrimp (peeled and deveined)
- 2 tbsp butter or ghee
- 1 tsp Cajun seasoning
- 1/2 tsp sea salt
- 1/4 tsp black pepper
- 1 clove garlic, minced (optional)

Instructions:
1. Pat the shrimp dry with paper towels to remove any excess moisture. In a small bowl, toss the shrimp with Cajun seasoning, sea salt, and black pepper until evenly coated.
2. In a large skillet, melt the butter or ghee over medium heat until it starts to foam. If using garlic, add it to the skillet and sauté for about 1 minute until fragrant.
3. Add the seasoned shrimp to the skillet and sauté for 2-3 minutes on each side, or until they turn pink and opaque. Remove the shrimp from the skillet and serve hot, drizzled with any remaining butter or ghee from the pan.

Nutritional Values: Calories: 180 kcal; **Protein:** 24g; **Fat:** 12g; **Carbohydrates:** 0g; **Sodium:** 550mg

GRILLED SHRIMP SKEWERS RECIPE

Preparation Time: 10 minutes
Cooking Time: 6-8 minutes
Portions: 1 person
Ingredients:
- 6 large shrimp (peeled and deveined)
- 1 tbsp olive oil
- 1/2 tsp sea salt
- 1/4 tsp black pepper
- 1/4 tsp garlic powder
- 1/4 tsp paprika (optional)

Instructions:
1. Preheat your grill to medium-high heat (about 400°F). In a small bowl, toss the shrimp with olive oil, sea salt, black pepper, garlic powder, and paprika (if using) until evenly coated.
2. Thread the shrimp onto skewers, making sure they are secure and evenly spaced.
3. Place the shrimp skewers on the preheated grill. Grill for 2-3 minutes on each side, or until the shrimp are pink, opaque, and have grill marks.
4. Remove the shrimp skewers from the grill and let them rest for 1-2 minutes. Serve the grilled shrimp skewers hot, optionally drizzled with additional olive oil or a squeeze of lemon.

Nutritional Values: Calories: 160 kcal; **Protein:** 24g; **Fat:** 7g; **Carbohydrates:** 0g; **Sodium:** 480mg

SAUTEED SHRIMP WITH BUTTER RECIPE

Preparation Time: 5 minutes
Cooking Time: 5-7 minutes
Portions: 1 person
Ingredients:
- 6 large shrimp (peeled and deveined)
- 2 tbsp butter
- 1/2 tsp sea salt
- 1/4 tsp black pepper
- 1/2 tsp garlic powder
- 1 tsp lemon juice (optional)

Instructions:
1. Pat the shrimp dry with paper towels to remove any excess moisture.
2. In a large skillet, melt the butter over medium heat until it starts to foam.
3. Add the shrimp to the skillet in a single layer. Sprinkle with sea salt, black pepper, and garlic powder. Sauté the shrimp for 2-3 minutes on each side, or until they turn pink and opaque.
4. If using, add the lemon juice to the skillet in the last minute of cooking and toss the shrimp to coat them evenly.
5. Remove the skillet from heat and let the shrimp rest for 1-2 minutes to absorb the flavors.
6. Serve the sautéed shrimp hot, drizzled with any remaining butter from the skillet.

Nutritional Values: Calories: 180 kcal; **Protein:** 24g; **Fat:** 10g; **Carbohydrates:** 0g; **Sodium:** 500mg

SPICY GARLIC SHRIMP RECIPE

Preparation Time: 5 minutes
Cooking Time: 5-7 minutes
Portions: 1 person
Ingredients:
- 6 large shrimp (peeled and deveined)
- 2 tbsp ghee or butter
- 2 cloves garlic, minced
- 1/2 tsp sea salt
- 1/4 tsp black pepper
- 1/4 tsp cayenne pepper (adjust to taste)

Instructions:
1. Pat the shrimp dry with paper towels to remove any excess moisture.
2. In a large skillet, melt the ghee or butter over medium heat until it starts to foam.
3. Add the minced garlic to the skillet and sauté for about 1 minute until fragrant, being careful not to burn the garlic.
4. Add the shrimp to the skillet and sprinkle with sea salt, black pepper, and cayenne pepper. Sauté the shrimp for 2-3 minutes on each side, or until they turn pink and opaque.
5. Toss the shrimp in the skillet to coat them evenly with the spicy garlic butter.
6. Remove the shrimp from the skillet and serve hot, drizzled with any remaining spicy garlic butter from the pan.

Nutritional Values: Calories: 190 kcal; **Protein:** 24g; **Fat:** 12g; **Carbohydrates:** 0g; **Sodium:** 520mg

SHELLFISH RECIPES

BACON-WRAPPED SCALLOPS RECIPE

Preparation Time: 10 minutes
Cooking Time: 12-15 minutes
Portions: 1 person
Ingredients:
- 4 large scallops
- 4 slices of bacon
- 1/2 tsp sea salt
- 1/4 tsp black pepper
- 1 tbsp butter (for basting)
- 1/4 tsp garlic powder (optional)

Instructions:
1. Preheat your oven to 400°F. Partially cook the bacon slices in a skillet over medium heat for about 4 minutes, until they start to render fat but are still pliable. Remove from the skillet and let them cool slightly.
2. Season the scallops with sea salt, black pepper, and optional garlic powder. Wrap each scallop with a slice of bacon and secure it with a toothpick.
3. Place the bacon-wrapped scallops on a baking sheet. Bake in the preheated oven for 12-15 minutes, turning once halfway through, until the bacon is crispy and the scallops are cooked through. In the last few minutes of baking, melt the butter in a small saucepan.
4. Remove the bacon-wrapped scallops from the oven, let them cool slightly, and serve hot.

Nutritional Values: Calories: 280 kcal; **Protein:** 20g; **Fat:** 20g; **Carbohydrates:** 0g; **Sodium:** 650mg

GRILLED OYSTERS RECIPE

Preparation Time: 5 minutes
Cooking Time: 5-7 minutes
Portions: 1 person
Ingredients:
- 6 fresh oysters, in the shell
- 2 tbsp butter, melted
- 1/2 tsp sea salt
- 1/4 tsp black pepper
- 1 clove garlic, minced (optional)
- 1 tsp lemon juice (optional)

Instructions:
1. Preheat your grill to medium-high heat (about 400°F). Scrub the oysters clean under cold water. Carefully shuck the oysters, leaving them in the half shell.
2. In a small bowl, mix the melted butter with sea salt, black pepper, and minced garlic (if using). Add the lemon juice to the butter mixture if desired.
3. Place the oysters directly on the grill with the shell side down. Spoon the butter mixture over each oyster, ensuring they are evenly coated. Grill for 5-7 minutes, or until the oysters are plump and the butter is bubbling. Carefully remove the oysters from the grill using tongs. Serve the grilled oysters hot, optionally garnished with a squeeze of additional lemon juice.

Nutritional Values: Calories: 150 kcal; **Protein:** 8g; **Fat:** 12g; **Carbohydrates:** 0g; **Sodium:** 350mg

LEMON BUTTER SCALLOPS RECIPE

Preparation Time: 5 minutes
Cooking Time: 5-7 minutes
Portions: 1 person
Ingredients:
- 6 large scallops
- 2 tbsp butter
- 1 tsp lemon juice
- 1/2 tsp sea salt
- 1/4 tsp black pepper
- 1/4 tsp garlic powder (optional)

Instructions:
1. Pat the scallops dry with paper towels to remove any excess moisture. Season both sides with sea salt, black pepper, and garlic powder (if using). In a large skillet, melt the butter over medium-high heat until it starts to foam.
2. Place the scallops in the skillet, making sure not to overcrowd them. Sear the scallops for 2-3 minutes on each side until they develop a golden-brown crust.
3. Reduce the heat to low and add the lemon juice to the skillet. Spoon the lemon butter sauce over the scallops to coat them evenly.
4. Continue to cook for an additional 1-2 minutes until the scallops are cooked through and opaque. Remove the scallops from the skillet and serve hot, drizzled with the remaining lemon butter sauce.

Nutritional Values: Calories: 220 kcal; **Protein:** 20g; **Fat:** 15g; **Carbohydrates:** 0g; **Sodium:** 550mg

PAN-FRIED CLAMS RECIPE

Preparation Time: 5 minutes
Cooking Time: 10 minutes
Portions: 1 person
Ingredients:
- 12 small clams, cleaned and scrubbed
- 2 tbsp ghee or butter
- 1/2 tsp sea salt
- 1/4 tsp black pepper
- 1/4 tsp garlic powder (optional)
- 1 tsp lemon juice (optional)

Instructions:
1. Ensure the clams are clean and scrubbed to remove any sand or grit. Pat them dry with a paper towel.
2. In a large skillet, melt the ghee or butter over medium heat until it starts to foam.
3. Season the clams with sea salt, black pepper, and garlic powder (if using).
4. Add the clams to the skillet, placing them in a single layer. Cook for 5-7 minutes, shaking the pan occasionally, until the clams open up. Discard any clams that do not open.
5. If using, drizzle the lemon juice over the clams in the last minute of cooking.
6. Remove the clams from the skillet and serve hot, optionally drizzled with any remaining pan juices.

Nutritional Values: Calories: 180 kcal; **Protein:** 16g; **Fat:** 12g; **Carbohydrates:** 0g; **Sodium:** 460mg

SEAFOOD MEDLEY IN GARLIC BUTTER RECIPE

Preparation Time: 5 minutes
Cooking Time: 10 minutes
Portions: 1 person
Ingredients:
- 2 oz shrimp (peeled and deveined)
- 2 oz scallops
- 2 oz clams (cleaned and scrubbed)
- 3 tbsp butter
- 2 cloves garlic, minced
- 1/2 tsp sea salt
- 1/4 tsp black pepper

Instructions:
1. Pat the shrimp, scallops, and clams dry with paper towels to remove any excess moisture.
2. In a large skillet, melt the butter over medium heat until it starts to foam.
3. Add the minced garlic to the skillet and sauté for about 1 minute until fragrant, being careful not to burn the garlic. Add the shrimp, scallops, and clams to the skillet. Season with sea salt and black pepper.
4. Cook for 5-7 minutes, stirring occasionally, until the shrimp are pink and opaque, the scallops are cooked through, and the clams have opened. Discard any clams that do not open.
5. Remove the seafood from the skillet and serve hot, drizzled with the garlic butter sauce from the pan.

Nutritional Values: Calories: 280 kcal; **Protein:** 28g; **Fat:** 18g; **Carbohydrates:** 0g; **Sodium:** 620mg

CHAPTER 9: EGG RECIPES

BREAKFAST RECIPES

BACON AND EGG SCRAMBLE RECIPE

Preparation Time: 5 minutes
Cooking Time: 10 minutes
Portions: 1 person
Ingredients:
- 2 large eggs
- 2 slices of bacon
- 1 tbsp butter
- 1/4 tsp sea salt and 1/4 tsp black pepper

Instructions:
1. In a skillet over medium heat, cook the bacon slices until crispy, about 5-7 minutes. Remove the bacon from the skillet and place it on a paper towel to drain. Once cooled, crumble the bacon into small pieces. In a small bowl, whisk the eggs with sea salt and black pepper until well combined. In the same skillet used for the bacon, melt the butter over medium heat. Pour the egg mixture into the skillet. Gently stir the eggs with a spatula, cooking until they are softly scrambled, about 3-4 minutes.
2. Once the eggs are nearly set, add the crumbled bacon to the skillet. Continue to cook, stirring until the eggs are fully cooked and the bacon is evenly distributed.

Nutritional Values: Calories: 320 kcal; **Protein:** 18g; **Fat:** 28g; **Carbohydrates:** 1g; **Sodium:** 670mg

EGG AND SAUSAGE BREAKFAST SKILLET RECIPE

Preparation Time: 5 minutes
Cooking Time: 10-12 minutes
Portions: 1 person
Ingredients:
- 2 large eggs
- 2 oz ground pork sausage
- 1 tbsp butter or ghee
- 1/4 tsp sea salt and 1/4 tsp black pepper
- 1/4 tsp garlic powder (optional)

Instructions:
1. In a skillet over medium heat, cook the ground pork sausage until browned and cooked through, about 5-7 minutes. Remove the cooked sausage from the skillet and set aside. In a small bowl, whisk the eggs with sea salt, black pepper, and garlic powder (if using) until well combined. In the same skillet used for the sausage, melt the butter or ghee over medium heat. Pour the egg mixture into the skillet.
2. Gently stir the eggs with a spatula, cooking until they are softly scrambled, about 3-4 minutes. Once the eggs are nearly set, add the cooked sausage back into the skillet. Continue to cook, stirring until the eggs are fully cooked and the sausage is evenly distributed. Remove the skillet from heat and serve the egg and sausage mixture hot.

Nutritional Values: Calories: 340 kcal; **Protein:** 22g; **Fat:** 28g; **Carbohydrates:** 1g; **Sodium:** 750mg

EGGS BENEDICT CARNIVORE STYLE RECIPE

Preparation Time: 10 minutes
Cooking Time: 10-12 minutes
Portions: 1 person
Ingredients:
- 2 large eggs
- 2 slices of bacon
- 1 slice of ham (about 2 oz)
- 2 tbsp butter (for hollandaise sauce)
- 1/4 tsp sea salt and 1/4 tsp black pepper

Instructions:
1. In a skillet over medium heat, cook the bacon slices until crispy, about 5-7 minutes. Remove the bacon from the skillet and place it on a paper towel to drain. In the same skillet, lightly fry the ham slice for 1-2 minutes on each side until warmed through and slightly browned.
2. In a small saucepan, melt 2 tbsp of butter over low heat. Once melted, remove from heat and let cool slightly. In a small bowl, whisk one egg yolk while slowly drizzling in the melted butter until the mixture thickens into a hollandaise sauce. Season with sea salt and black pepper.
3. In a small saucepan, bring water to a gentle simmer (not boiling). Crack the eggs into the water and poach for about 3-4 minutes, until the whites are set but the yolks are still runny. Remove the eggs with a slotted spoon and drain any excess water. Place the ham slice on a plate. Top with the poached eggs and crispy bacon. Spoon the hollandaise sauce over the eggs and bacon, ensuring it's evenly distributed. Serve immediately while warm, garnished with additional black pepper if desired.

Nutritional Values: Calories: 450 kcal; **Protein:** 30g; **Fat:** 36g; **Carbohydrates:** 1g; **Sodium:** 980mg

OMELETTE WITH BACON AND CHEESE RECIPE

Preparation Time: 5 minutes
Cooking Time: 10 minutes
Portions: 1 person
Ingredients:
- 2 large eggs
- 2 slices of bacon
- 1/4 cup shredded cheddar cheese
- 1 tbsp butter
- 1/4 tsp sea salt and 1/4 tsp black pepper

Instructions:
1. In a skillet over medium heat, cook the bacon slices until crispy, about 5-7 minutes. Remove the bacon from the skillet and place it on a paper towel to drain. Once cooled, crumble the bacon into small pieces. In a small bowl, whisk the eggs with sea salt and black pepper until well combined. In the same skillet used for the bacon, melt the butter over medium heat.
2. Pour the egg mixture into the skillet and let it cook undisturbed for about 1-2 minutes, until the edges start to set. Sprinkle the crumbled bacon and shredded cheddar cheese over one half of the omelette.
3. Carefully fold the omelette in half to cover the filling. Continue to cook for another 2-3 minutes, until the cheese is melted and the eggs are fully cooked.

Nutritional Values: Calories: 350 kcal; **Protein:** 22g; **Fat:** 29g; **Carbohydrates:** 1g; **Sodium:** 780mg

STEAK AND EGG BREAKFAST BOWL RECIPE

Preparation Time: 5 minutes
Cooking Time: 10-12 minutes
Portions: 1 person
Ingredients:
- 4 oz steak (your choice of cut, such as ribeye or sirloin)
- 2 large eggs
- 1 tbsp ghee or butter
- 1/4 tsp sea salt and 1/4 tsp black pepper
- 1/4 tsp garlic powder (optional)

Instructions:
1. Heat a skillet over medium-high heat and add 1/2 tbsp of ghee or butter. Season the steak with sea salt, black pepper, and garlic powder (if using). Cook the steak for 3-4 minutes on each side, or until it reaches your desired level of doneness.
2. Remove the steak from the skillet and let it rest for a few minutes before slicing it into thin strips.
3. In the same skillet, add the remaining 1/2 tbsp of ghee or butter. Crack the eggs into the skillet and cook them to your preference (sunny-side-up, over-easy, scrambled, etc.). Season with a pinch of sea salt and black pepper.
4. Place the steak strips in a bowl. Add the cooked eggs on top of the steak. For added flavor, drizzle any remaining pan juices over the steak and eggs.
5. Serve the breakfast bowl hot, with additional sea salt and black pepper to taste.

Nutritional Values: Calories: 400 kcal; **Protein:** 36g; **Fat:** 28g; **Carbohydrates:** 0g; **Sodium:** 620mg

LUNCH AND DINNER RECIPES

BEEF AND EGG STIR-FRY RECIPE

Preparation Time: 5 minutes
Cooking Time: 10 minutes
Portions: 1 person
Ingredients:
- 4 oz ground beef
- 2 large eggs
- 1 tbsp butter or ghee
- 1/4 tsp sea salt and 1/4 tsp black pepper
- 1/4 tsp garlic powder (optional)

Instructions:
1. Heat a skillet over medium heat and add the ground beef. Season with sea salt, black pepper, and garlic powder (if using). Cook the beef, breaking it up with a spatula, until browned and fully cooked, about 5-7 minutes. In a small bowl, whisk the eggs until well combined.
2. In the same skillet with the cooked ground beef, push the beef to one side and melt the butter on the other side of the skillet. Pour the whisked eggs into the melted butter. Let the eggs cook for 1-2 minutes, then gently stir them, scrambling the eggs and mixing them with the ground beef. Continue to cook until the eggs are fully set and mixed evenly with the ground beef, about 2-3 minutes. Remove the beef and egg stir-fry from the skillet and serve hot.

Nutritional Values: Calories: 350 kcal; **Protein:** 28g; **Fat:** 26g; **Carbohydrates:** 0g; **Sodium:** 400mg

CHEESY EGG-STUFFED MEATBALLS RECIPE

Preparation Time: 10 minutes
Cooking Time: 20 minutes
Portions: 1 person
Ingredients:
- 4 oz ground beef
- 1 large egg
- 1/4 cup shredded cheddar cheese
- 1/2 tsp sea salt and 1/4 tsp black pepper
- 1/4 tsp garlic powder (optional)

Instructions:
1. Preheat your oven to 375°F (190°C). In a bowl, combine the ground beef, sea salt, black pepper, and garlic powder (if using). Mix until well combined. Divide the meat mixture into two equal portions. Flatten each portion into a disc and place half of the shredded cheddar cheese in the center of each disc. Fold the meat around the cheese, shaping it into a ball, ensuring the cheese is fully enclosed.
2. Place the meatballs on a baking sheet lined with parchment paper. Bake in the preheated oven for 15 minutes. While the meatballs are baking, cook the egg to your preference (hard-boiled, poached, or soft-boiled). If hard-boiled, slice the egg in half.
3. Once the meatballs are cooked, remove them from the oven. Serve the meatballs with the cooked egg, garnishing with additional cheese if desired.

Nutritional Values: Calories: 400 kcal; **Protein:** 32g; **Fat:** 30g; **Carbohydrates:** 1g; **Sodium:** 600mg

CHICKEN AND EGG DROP SOUP RECIPE

Preparation Time: 5 minutes
Cooking Time: 15 minutes
Portions: 1 person
Ingredients:
- 1 cup chicken broth (preferably homemade or low-sodium)
- 2 oz cooked shredded chicken
- 1 large egg
- 1 tbsp butter or ghee
- 1/4 tsp sea salt (adjust to taste)
- 1/4 tsp black pepper

Instructions:
1. In a small saucepan, bring the chicken broth to a gentle boil over medium heat.
2. Add the shredded chicken to the broth. Reduce the heat to low and let it simmer for 3-5 minutes, allowing the flavors to meld together. In a small bowl, whisk the egg until well beaten. Slowly pour the beaten egg into the simmering broth in a thin stream while gently stirring the soup in a circular motion. The egg will cook instantly, forming delicate ribbons.
3. Add the butter or ghee to the soup, stirring until melted and incorporated. Season with sea salt and black pepper to taste.
4. Pour the soup into a bowl and serve hot.

Nutritional Values: Calories: 220 kcal; **Protein:** 22g; **Fat:** 15g; **Carbohydrates:** 0g; **Sodium:** 800mg

SALMON AND EGG CASSEROLE RECIPE

Preparation Time: 10 minutes
Cooking Time: 25 minutes
Portions: 1 person
Ingredients:
- 2 oz canned salmon (drained)
- 2 large eggs
- 1/4 cup shredded cheddar cheese
- 1 tbsp butter (for greasing)
- 1/4 tsp sea salt
- 1/4 tsp black pepper

Instructions:
1. Preheat your oven to 350°F (175°C). Grease a small baking dish with butter.
2. In a bowl, whisk the eggs until well beaten. Season with sea salt and black pepper.
3. Spread the drained canned salmon evenly at the bottom of the greased baking dish. Pour the beaten eggs over the salmon.
4. Sprinkle the shredded cheddar cheese evenly over the top of the egg and salmon mixture.
5. Place the baking dish in the preheated oven and bake for 20-25 minutes, or until the eggs are fully set and the cheese is melted and golden.
6. Remove the casserole from the oven and let it cool slightly before serving.

Nutritional Values: Calories: 330 kcal; **Protein:** 30g; **Fat:** 22g; **Carbohydrates:** 1g; **Sodium:** 600mg

TURKEY AND EGG BAKE RECIPE

Preparation Time: 10 minutes
Cooking Time: 25 minutes
Portions: 1 person
Ingredients:
- 2 oz ground turkey
- 2 large eggs
- 1/4 cup shredded cheddar cheese
- 1 tbsp butter (for greasing)
- 1/4 tsp sea salt
- 1/4 tsp black pepper

Instructions:
1. Preheat your oven to 350°F (175°C). Grease a small baking dish with butter.
2. In a skillet over medium heat, cook the ground turkey until browned and fully cooked, about 5-7 minutes. Season with sea salt and black pepper and set aside.
3. In a bowl, whisk the eggs until well beaten.
4. Spread the cooked turkey evenly in the greased baking dish. Pour the beaten eggs over the turkey. Sprinkle the shredded cheddar cheese evenly on top.
5. Place the baking dish in the preheated oven and bake for 20-25 minutes, or until the eggs are fully set and the cheese is melted and slightly browned.
6. Remove the turkey and egg bake from the oven, let it cool slightly, and serve hot.

Nutritional Values: Calories: 350 kcal; **Protein:** 30g; **Fat:** 24g; **Carbohydrates:** 1g; **Sodium:** 580mg

SNACKS AND SIDES

CREAMY EGG SALAD RECIPE

Preparation Time: 10 minutes
Cooking Time: 10 minutes (for boiling eggs)
Portions: 1 person
Ingredients:
- 2 large eggs
- 1 tbsp mayonnaise (carnivore-friendly)
- 1 tsp mustard (optional)
- 1/4 tsp sea salt and 1/4 tsp black pepper
- 1 tbsp butter (optional, for added creaminess)

Instructions:
1. Place the eggs in a saucepan and cover with cold water. Bring to a boil over medium-high heat. Once boiling, reduce the heat to low and let the eggs simmer for 9-10 minutes.
2. Drain the hot water and place the eggs in a bowl of ice water to cool for a few minutes. Once cooled, peel the eggs and chop them into small pieces. In a mixing bowl, combine the chopped eggs, mayonnaise, and mustard (if using). Mix well until the eggs are evenly coated. Add sea salt and black pepper to taste. For added creaminess, you can also mix in the butter, softened to room temperature.
3. Stir the egg salad until all ingredients are fully combined. Serve immediately or chill in the refrigerator for a few minutes before serving.

Nutritional Values: Calories: 220 kcal; **Protein:** 12g; **Fat:** 18g; **Carbohydrates:** 0g; **Sodium:** 400mg

EGG AND SAUSAGE MUFFIN CUPS RECIPE

Preparation Time: 10 minutes
Cooking Time: 20 minutes
Portions: 1 person (makes 2 muffin cups)
Ingredients:
- 2 large eggs
- 2 oz ground sausage
- 1/4 cup shredded cheddar cheese
- 1 tbsp butter or ghee (for greasing)
- 1/4 tsp sea salt and 1/4 tsp black pepper

Instructions:
1. Preheat your oven to 350°F (175°C). Grease two compartments of a muffin tin with butter or ghee. In a skillet over medium heat, cook the ground sausage until browned and fully cooked, about 5-7 minutes. Remove from heat and set aside.
2. In a bowl, whisk the eggs until well beaten. Season with sea salt and black pepper.
3. Evenly divide the cooked sausage between the two greased muffin compartments. Pour the beaten eggs over the sausage in each compartment. Sprinkle shredded cheddar cheese on top of each muffin cup.
4. Place the muffin tin in the preheated oven and bake for 15-20 minutes, or until the eggs are fully set and the cheese is melted and slightly browned. Remove the muffin cups from the oven and let them cool slightly before serving.

Nutritional Values: Calories: 280 kcal; **Protein:** 22g; **Fat:** 22g; **Carbohydrates:** 0g; **Sodium:** 550mg

MINI EGG FRITTATAS RECIPE

Preparation Time: 10 minutes
Cooking Time: 20 minutes
Portions: 1 person (makes 2 mini frittatas)
Ingredients:
- 2 large eggs
- 2 slices of bacon, cooked and crumbled
- 1/4 cup shredded cheddar cheese
- 1 tbsp butter or ghee (for greasing)
- 1/4 tsp sea salt and 1/4 tsp black pepper

Instructions:
1. Preheat your oven to 350°F (175°C). Grease two compartments of a muffin tin with butter or ghee. In a bowl, whisk the eggs until well beaten. Season with sea salt and black pepper.
2. Evenly divide the crumbled bacon between the two greased muffin compartments. Pour the beaten eggs over the bacon in each compartment. Sprinkle shredded cheddar cheese on top of each frittata.
3. Place the muffin tin in the preheated oven and bake for 15-20 minutes, or until the eggs are fully set and the cheese is melted and slightly browned.
4. Remove the muffin tin from the oven and let the frittatas cool for a few minutes before carefully removing them from the tin.

Nutritional Values: Calories: 280 kcal; **Protein:** 20g; **Fat:** 22g; **Carbohydrates:** 0g; **Sodium:** 550mg

SOFT-BOILED EGGS WITH HERB BUTTER RECIPE

Preparation Time: 5 minutes
Cooking Time: 7 minutes
Portions: 1 person
Ingredients:
- 2 large eggs
- 1 tbsp butter
- 1/4 tsp sea salt
- 1/4 tsp black pepper
- 1/4 tsp dried rosemary (or your preferred herb)
- 1/4 tsp dried thyme

Instructions:
1. Fill a small saucepan with enough water to cover the eggs. Bring the water to a boil over medium-high heat. Once boiling, gently lower the eggs into the water using a spoon. Boil the eggs for exactly 6-7 minutes for soft yolks.
2. While the eggs are boiling, melt the butter in a small pan over low heat. Stir in the rosemary and thyme, then season with sea salt and black pepper.
3. After boiling, immediately transfer the eggs to a bowl of ice water to stop the cooking process. Let them cool for about 1-2 minutes, then carefully peel the eggs.
4. Place the peeled soft-boiled eggs in a small dish. Drizzle the herb butter over the eggs.
5. Sprinkle additional sea salt and black pepper to taste if desired. Serve immediately while warm, allowing the yolk to mix with the herb butter as you cut into the eggs.

Nutritional Values: Calories: 200 kcal; **Protein:** 12g; **Fat:** 17g; **Carbohydrates:** 1g; **Sodium:** 300mg

SPICY DEVILED EGGS RECIPE

Preparation Time: 10 minutes
Cooking Time: 10 minutes (for boiling eggs)
Portions: 1 person
Ingredients:
- 2 large eggs
- 1 tbsp mayonnaise (carnivore-friendly)
- 1/4 tsp cayenne pepper
- 1/4 tsp sea salt
- 1/4 tsp black pepper
- 1/4 tsp paprika (for garnish)

Instructions:
1. Place the eggs in a saucepan and cover them with cold water. Bring the water to a boil over medium-high heat. Once boiling, reduce the heat to low and let the eggs simmer for 9-10 minutes. Drain the hot water and place the eggs in a bowl of ice water to cool for a few minutes. Once cooled, peel the eggs.
2. Slice the peeled eggs in half lengthwise and gently remove the yolks. Place the yolks in a small bowl and mash them with a fork. Add the mayonnaise, cayenne pepper, sea salt, and black pepper to the mashed yolks. Mix until smooth and well combined.
3. Spoon or pipe the yolk mixture back into the egg white halves.
4. Sprinkle the tops of the filled eggs with a pinch of paprika for added flavor and color.
5. Serve the spicy deviled eggs immediately or refrigerate them until ready to serve.

Nutritional Values: Calories: 160 kcal; **Protein:** 10g; **Fat:** 13g; **Carbohydrates:** 0g; **Sodium:** 350mg

PART 3: SUPPORTING YOUR CARNIVORE JOURNEY

Embarking on the Carnivore Diet is not just about changing what you eat; it's about embracing a new way of living that supports your overall well-being. In Part 3, we'll explore the essential tools, strategies, and mindsets that will help you thrive on this journey. From managing social situations to understanding your body's signals, this chapter provides the guidance you need to navigate challenges and stay motivated. Together, we'll build the foundation for long-term success, ensuring that you not only achieve your goals but also enjoy the process of transforming your health.

CHAPTER 10: SUPPLEMENTING ON THE CARNIVORE DIET

DO YOU NEED SUPPLEMENTS? THE DEBATE

When it comes to the Carnivore Diet, one of the most common questions is whether or not you need to take supplements. This topic is a source of considerable debate within the carnivore community, with opinions ranging from the belief that all necessary nutrients can be obtained exclusively from animal foods to the perspective that certain supplements might be beneficial or even necessary. To help you make an informed decision, let's delve into the arguments on both sides and explore what the science and real-world experience tell us.

The Argument for a Whole Foods-Only Approach

One of the central tenets of the Carnivore Diet is that it's a return to a more natural way of eating—one that our ancestors thrived on long before the advent of modern agriculture and processed foods. Proponents of a whole foods-only approach argue that if you're consuming a varied diet of nutrient-dense animal products, you're providing your body with everything it needs to function optimally. This includes essential amino acids, fats, vitamins, and minerals that are all available in highly bioavailable forms in animal foods.

For example, red meat, particularly organ meats like liver, is a powerhouse of nutrients such as vitamin A, B vitamins, iron, zinc, and selenium. Fatty fish provides essential omega-3 fatty acids, which are crucial for brain health and reducing inflammation. Eggs and dairy products contribute additional nutrients like choline, calcium, and vitamin D. In this view, the Carnivore Diet, when properly executed, can supply all the nutrients your body needs without the need for external supplementation.

Moreover, the argument against supplementation often includes the idea that supplements can sometimes do more harm than good. Synthetic vitamins and minerals may not be absorbed as effectively as those found in whole foods, and there's a risk of over-supplementation, which can lead to imbalances and even toxicity. The natural synergy of nutrients in whole foods is something that supplements cannot replicate, and disrupting this balance could potentially negate some of the benefits of the diet.

The Case for Strategic Supplementation

On the other hand, some advocates within the carnivore community recognize that modern life presents unique challenges that our ancestors didn't face, which might justify the use of certain supplements. Factors such as soil depletion, food processing, and lifestyle choices can impact the nutrient density of the foods we consume today, even those on a strict Carnivore Diet. Additionally, individual variability in digestion, absorption, and metabolic needs can mean that some people may benefit from targeted supplementation.

For example, vitamin D is a nutrient that, while present in some animal foods like fatty fish and egg yolks, is primarily obtained through sun exposure. Given that many people spend the majority of their time indoors or live in regions with limited sunlight, a vitamin D supplement might be necessary to maintain optimal levels, particularly during the winter months.

Magnesium is another nutrient that, despite being present in animal foods, can be challenging to obtain in sufficient quantities, especially given the depletion of magnesium in modern soils. Magnesium is essential for a wide range of bodily functions, including muscle and nerve function, blood sugar control, and the production of proteins and DNA. Some people on the Carnivore Diet find that supplementing with magnesium helps alleviate issues like muscle cramps, constipation, or sleep disturbances.

Omega-3 fatty acids, while available in fatty fish and some grass-fed meats, may also be worth considering, particularly if your diet is heavily weighted towards meats that are higher in omega-6 fatty acids. Maintaining a balanced omega-3 to omega-6 ratio is important for reducing inflammation and supporting heart and brain health.

Finally, while the Carnivore Diet is often praised for its ability to reduce or eliminate digestive issues, some individuals may benefit from digestive support, especially during the initial transition period. Digestive enzymes or hydrochloric acid (HCL) supplements can assist with the breakdown of protein and fat, easing the digestive process as your body adapts to this way of eating.

FINDING THE RIGHT BALANCE

Ultimately, the decision to supplement on the Carnivore Diet should be based on a careful assessment of your individual needs, goals, and lifestyle factors. If you're thriving on a diverse diet of animal products and feel confident in your nutrient intake, you may find that you don't need supplements at all. However, if you have specific health concerns, live in an environment that limits your exposure to certain nutrients (like vitamin D from sunlight), or notice signs of potential deficiencies, strategic supplementation might be beneficial.

It's also important to remember that supplementation should not be seen as a replacement for a well-rounded diet. The foundation of your nutrition should always be whole, nutrient-dense animal foods, with supplements playing a supporting role if needed.

Consulting with a healthcare professional who understands the Carnivore Diet can also help you make informed decisions about whether supplementation is right for you.

Essential Nutrients and How to Get Them

On the Carnivore Diet, your nutrition is derived entirely from animal-based foods, making it crucial to understand where to obtain the essential nutrients your body needs to thrive. While this way of eating might seem restrictive at first glance, animal products are, in fact, rich sources of nearly all the nutrients necessary for optimal health. By carefully selecting a variety of meats, organs, and other animal-derived foods, you can ensure that you're meeting your nutritional needs without relying on plant-based sources or supplements.

Protein: The Building Block of Life

Protein is the cornerstone of the Carnivore Diet and is essential for maintaining muscle mass, repairing tissues, producing enzymes and hormones, and supporting overall health. Animal products provide complete proteins, meaning they contain all nine essential amino acids that your body cannot produce on its own.

Where to Get It:

- **Beef, Pork, and Poultry:** These meats are excellent sources of high-quality protein. Cuts like ribeye, sirloin, chicken thighs, and pork chops are not only delicious but also packed with the amino acids your body needs.
- **Fish and Seafood:** Salmon, tuna, cod, and shellfish offer a leaner option while still delivering a potent protein punch. Fatty fish like salmon also provide the added benefit of omega-3 fatty acids.
- **Eggs:** A versatile and nutrient-dense option, eggs are a powerhouse of protein and also contain essential vitamins like B12 and D.

Fats: Essential for Energy and Cellular Health

Fats are a primary energy source on the Carnivore Diet, especially since carbohydrates are virtually nonexistent in this way of eating. Fats support hormone production, cell membrane integrity, and the absorption of fat-soluble vitamins (A, D, E, and K).

Where to Get It:
- **Fatty Cuts of Meat:** Opt for cuts like ribeye, pork belly, and lamb chops, which are rich in healthy fats. These fats not only provide energy but also help keep you satiated.
- **Butter and Ghee:** These animal fats are rich in saturated fats and can be used in cooking or as a topping on meats.
- **Bone Marrow:** An often-overlooked delicacy, bone marrow is incredibly nutrient-dense and provides both fats and essential fatty acids.

Vitamin B12: Crucial for Energy and Nervous System Health

Vitamin B12 is vital for red blood cell formation, DNA synthesis, and the proper functioning of the nervous system. It is one of the nutrients that is exclusively found in animal products, making it especially important on the Carnivore Diet.

Where to Get It:
- **Liver and Organ Meats:** Beef liver is one of the richest sources of vitamin B12. Including organ meats in your diet can significantly boost your intake of this essential nutrient.
- **Red Meat:** Beef, lamb, and pork are also excellent sources of B12, making regular consumption of these meats an easy way to meet your needs.
- **Fish and Shellfish:** Clams, trout, and salmon are particularly high in B12, offering a great alternative to red meat.

Iron: For Oxygen Transport and Energy

Iron is critical for producing hemoglobin, the protein in red blood cells that carries oxygen throughout your body. The type of iron found in animal products, known as heme iron, is more easily absorbed by the body compared to non-heme iron found in plants.

Where to Get It:
- **Red Meat:** Beef, lamb, and venison are all rich in heme iron. Regular consumption of these meats can help maintain healthy iron levels.
- **Liver:** Beef liver is particularly high in iron and provides a concentrated source that can boost your intake.
- **Egg Yolks:** Although not as rich as red meat or liver, egg yolks still provide a good amount of heme iron.

Zinc: Supporting Immune Function and Cellular Metabolism

Zinc plays a vital role in immune function, protein synthesis, wound healing, and DNA synthesis. It's also crucial for proper taste and smell. Animal foods are among the best sources of bioavailable zinc.

Where to Get It:
- **Red Meat and Poultry:** Beef and chicken are excellent sources of zinc. Ground beef, in particular, can be an easy and affordable way to increase your zinc intake.
- **Shellfish:** Oysters are incredibly rich in zinc, providing far more than your daily requirement in just a few pieces. Other shellfish, like crab and shrimp, are also good sources.
- **Pork:** Pork, especially pork shoulder and chops, offers a solid amount of zinc.

Vitamin A: Essential for Vision and Immune Health

Vitamin A is crucial for maintaining healthy vision, supporting immune function, and ensuring proper cell growth. In animal products, vitamin A is found in its active form, retinol, which is easily absorbed and utilized by the body.

Where to Get It:
- **Liver:** Liver, particularly beef liver, is one of the richest sources of vitamin A. Just a small serving provides well over your daily requirement.
- **Egg Yolks:** Eggs, particularly those from pastured hens, contain retinol and are a convenient way to include vitamin A in your diet.
- **Dairy Products:** Full-fat dairy, such as butter and cream, also contains vitamin A in its active form.

Omega-3 Fatty Acids: Reducing Inflammation and Supporting Heart Health

Omega-3 fatty acids are essential fats that play a key role in reducing inflammation, supporting brain health, and promoting heart health. These fats are especially important on the Carnivore Diet, where maintaining a healthy balance of omega-3 to omega-6 is crucial.

Where to Get It:
- **Fatty Fish:** Salmon, mackerel, sardines, and herring are rich in omega-3 fatty acids, making them an essential part of the Carnivore Diet.
- **Grass-Fed Meats:** Meats from grass-fed animals tend to have higher levels of omega-3s compared to grain-fed animals.
- **Eggs:** Omega-3 enriched eggs, which come from hens fed a diet high in omega-3s, can be another good source.

Vitamin D: The Sunshine Vitamin

Vitamin D is crucial for bone health, immune function, and mood regulation. While it's primarily obtained through sun exposure, certain animal foods can also provide this essential vitamin.

Where to Get It:
- **Fatty Fish:** Salmon, mackerel, and sardines are excellent sources of vitamin D.
- **Egg Yolks:** Eggs, especially those from free-range hens, contain some vitamin D.
- **Liver:** Beef liver, while more known for vitamin A, also contains a small amount of vitamin D.

Calcium: Building Strong Bones and Teeth

Calcium is essential for building and maintaining strong bones and teeth, as well as for supporting nerve function and muscle contraction. While dairy products are the most well-known sources of calcium, there are other animal-based options as well.

Where to Get It:
- **Dairy Products:** Cheese, yogurt, and milk are rich in calcium. Full-fat dairy options are recommended on the Carnivore Diet for their additional nutrient content.
- **Bone-In Fish:** Sardines and salmon with bones are excellent non-dairy sources of calcium.
- **Bone Broth:** Made by simmering bones, bone broth is not only rich in calcium but also provides collagen and other important nutrients for joint health.

RECOMMENDED SUPPLEMENTS FOR CARNIVORE DIETERS

While the Carnivore Diet is designed to provide a comprehensive range of nutrients through animal-based foods, there are certain circumstances where supplementation might be beneficial or even necessary. These recommendations are not one-size-fits-all, but rather considerations based on individual needs, lifestyle factors, and potential gaps that might arise even in a well-structured carnivore regimen. Below, we'll explore some of the most commonly recommended supplements for those following the Carnivore Diet, explaining why they might be useful and how to incorporate them effectively.

1. Electrolytes: Balancing Sodium, Potassium, and Magnesium

One of the most important supplements to consider on the Carnivore Diet is electrolytes, particularly in the early stages of the diet when your body is adjusting to a lower intake of carbohydrates. Electrolytes are crucial for maintaining proper hydration, nerve function, and muscle contractions. The Carnivore Diet, by nature of being low in carbohydrates, often leads to a diuretic effect where your body excretes more water and, with it, essential electrolytes like sodium, potassium, and magnesium.

Why It's Important:
- **Sodium:** Sodium is essential for maintaining fluid balance, nerve transmission, and muscle function. On the Carnivore Diet, you may need to increase your sodium intake to compensate for the loss of sodium that occurs with reduced carbohydrate intake.
- **Potassium:** Potassium helps regulate heartbeat, muscle contractions, and nerve signals. It also balances the effects of sodium and can help prevent cramping.
- **Magnesium:** Magnesium plays a role in over 300 biochemical reactions in your body, including energy production, muscle

and nerve function, and blood pressure regulation.

Recommended Supplementation:
- **Electrolyte Powders or Tablets:** These are convenient options that typically contain a balanced mix of sodium, potassium, and magnesium. Look for products without added sugars or artificial ingredients.
- **Sodium:** Simply adding extra salt to your meals or drinking salt water (about half a teaspoon of sea salt in a glass of water) can help meet your sodium needs.
- **Magnesium Supplements:** Magnesium citrate, glycinate, or malate are well-absorbed forms of magnesium that can be taken as supplements to help prevent deficiencies, particularly if you're experiencing muscle cramps or sleep disturbances.

2. Vitamin D: The Sunshine Vitamin

Vitamin D is a fat-soluble vitamin that is crucial for bone health, immune function, and mood regulation. While it can be obtained from certain foods, the primary source of vitamin D is sunlight exposure. Given that many people spend a significant amount of time indoors or live in regions with limited sunlight, particularly during the winter months, vitamin D deficiency is common.

Why It's Important:
- **Bone Health:** Vitamin D is essential for calcium absorption and bone mineralization, helping to prevent osteoporosis and fractures.
- **Immune Function:** Vitamin D plays a critical role in supporting the immune system and has been linked to a reduced risk of chronic diseases.
- **Mood Regulation:** Adequate vitamin D levels are associated with improved mood and a lower risk of depression.

Recommended Supplementation:
- **Vitamin D3 Supplements:** Vitamin D3 (cholecalciferol) is the most effective form of vitamin D for raising blood levels. Depending on your location, skin type, and sun exposure, a supplement ranging from 1,000 to 5,000 IU per day is often recommended. It's best to get your levels checked and adjust your dosage accordingly.

3. Omega-3 Fatty Acids: Supporting Heart and Brain Health

Omega-3 fatty acids are essential fats that play a critical role in reducing inflammation, supporting heart health, and promoting cognitive function. While the Carnivore Diet can provide omega-3s through fatty fish and grass-fed meats, some individuals may still benefit from supplementation, particularly if their diet is lacking in these specific foods.

Why It's Important:
- **Anti-Inflammatory Effects:** Omega-3s help balance the inflammatory effects of omega-6 fatty acids, which are more prevalent in conventional grain-fed meats.
- **Heart Health:** Omega-3s are known to reduce triglycerides, lower blood pressure, and decrease the risk of heart disease.
- **Cognitive Function:** DHA, a type of omega-3, is crucial for brain health and has been linked to improved memory, mood, and mental clarity.

Recommended Supplementation:
- **Fish Oil Supplements:** A high-quality fish oil supplement that provides both EPA and DHA can help ensure you're getting enough omega-3s, especially if you don't eat fatty fish regularly. Aim for a daily dose that provides at least 1,000 mg of combined EPA and DHA.
- **Cod Liver Oil:** Another option is cod liver oil, which not only provides omega-3s but also contains vitamins A and D.

4. Magnesium: Supporting Muscle and Nerve Function

Magnesium, as mentioned earlier, is a mineral that plays a vital role in various bodily functions, from energy production to muscle relaxation. While it's found in small amounts in animal products, some people may require additional magnesium to meet their needs, particularly if they experience symptoms like muscle cramps, anxiety, or difficulty sleeping.

Why It's Important:
- **Energy Production:** Magnesium is involved in the production of ATP, the energy currency of the cell, which is crucial for maintaining stamina and vitality.
- **Muscle and Nerve Function:** Magnesium helps regulate muscle contractions and nerve signals, preventing cramps and spasms.
- **Relaxation and Sleep:** Magnesium has a calming effect on the nervous system, making it beneficial for reducing stress and improving sleep quality.

Recommended Supplementation:
- **Magnesium Glycinate or Citrate:** These forms of magnesium are well-absorbed and can be taken daily to support overall health. Start with a dose of 200-400 mg per day, and adjust based on your needs and tolerance.

5. Iodine: Supporting Thyroid Function

Iodine is an essential trace element that is critical for thyroid hormone production. These hormones regulate metabolism, energy levels, and many other important functions in the body. While iodine is present in seafood and iodized salt, some carnivores may still need to supplement, especially if they avoid processed foods that are often fortified with iodine.

Why It's Important:
- **Thyroid Health:** Iodine is necessary for the production of thyroid hormones, which regulate metabolic rate, energy production, and overall metabolic health.
- **Hormonal Balance:** Proper thyroid function is essential for maintaining hormonal balance and supporting overall health.

Recommended Supplementation:
- **Iodine Supplements:** If your diet is low in iodine-rich foods, consider a supplement. Kelp tablets or iodine drops can provide a natural source of iodine. The recommended daily intake is around 150 mcg, but it's important not to exceed this without medical guidance, as excessive iodine can have adverse effects on thyroid health.

6. Collagen: Supporting Joint and Skin Health

Collagen is the most abundant protein in the body and is a key component of connective tissues, including skin, joints, and bones. While the Carnivore Diet naturally provides some collagen through the consumption of skin, cartilage, and bone broths, a collagen supplement can help ensure adequate intake, especially for those concerned about joint health or skin elasticity.

Why It's Important:
- **Joint Health:** Collagen supports the integrity of cartilage, reducing joint pain and stiffness, particularly for those engaging in regular physical activity.
- **Skin Health:** Collagen helps maintain skin elasticity and hydration, reducing the appearance of wrinkles and promoting a youthful complexion.
- **Gut Health:** Collagen has been shown to support gut health by strengthening the gut lining, which can be beneficial for those with digestive issues.

Recommended Supplementation:
- **Collagen Peptides:** Collagen peptides are a highly bioavailable form of collagen that can be easily mixed into beverages or added to meals. A daily dose of 10-20 grams is typical for supporting joint, skin, and gut health.

CHAPTER 11: HYDRATION AND ELECTROLYTE BALANCE

THE IMPORTANCE OF HYDRATION ON THE CARNIVORE DIET

Hydration is a fundamental aspect of overall health, and it becomes even more critical when you're following the Carnivore Diet. This way of eating, which emphasizes high intake of protein and fats with minimal carbohydrates, can significantly alter your body's water balance and electrolyte needs. Understanding how to maintain proper hydration on the Carnivore Diet is essential for optimizing your health, performance, and well-being.

Why Hydration Needs Change on the Carnivore Diet?
When you reduce or eliminate carbohydrates from your diet, as you do on the Carnivore Diet, your body undergoes several physiological changes that directly impact your hydration status. Carbohydrates are stored in your muscles and liver as glycogen, which binds to water. For every gram of glycogen, approximately three grams of water are stored. When you reduce your carbohydrate intake, your glycogen stores deplete, and your body releases the associated water, leading to increased urination. This diuretic effect can result in a significant loss of fluids and electrolytes, particularly in the early stages of the diet.

Additionally, the Carnivore Diet's emphasis on protein and fats shifts your body's metabolism, which can also influence hydration. Protein metabolism generates urea, a waste product that requires adequate water for excretion through the kidneys. If you're not drinking enough water, this can put additional strain on your kidneys and may lead to dehydration or other complications.

Signs of Dehydration on the Carnivore Diet
Recognizing the signs of dehydration is crucial for maintaining your health on the Carnivore Diet. Some common symptoms of dehydration include:
- **Dry Mouth and Thirst:** Feeling unusually thirsty or having a dry mouth is a clear indication that your body needs more fluids.
- **Dark Urine:** Urine that is dark yellow or amber in color can signal dehydration. Ideally, your urine should be light yellow to clear.
- **Headaches:** Dehydration can lead to headaches or a feeling of lightheadedness, especially if electrolyte levels are imbalanced.
- **Fatigue:** Feeling unusually tired or lethargic may be a sign that you're not getting enough fluids and electrolytes.
- **Muscle Cramps:** Cramping in the muscles, particularly in the legs, can indicate a deficiency in sodium, potassium, or magnesium.
- **Dizziness:** Feeling dizzy or faint is a more severe sign of dehydration and requires immediate attention.

Strategies for Staying Hydrated
Maintaining proper hydration on the Carnivore Diet requires a proactive approach, particularly given the increased excretion of fluids and electrolytes. Here are some effective strategies to ensure you stay well-hydrated:
1. Drink Water Throughout the Day: Aim to drink water consistently throughout the day, rather than waiting until you feel thirsty. Start your day with a glass of water and continue to sip water regularly, especially before and after meals. The amount of water you need will vary depending on your body size, activity level, and climate, but a general guideline is to aim for at least 8-10 cups (64-80 ounces) of water per day, adjusting as needed based on your individual needs.
2. Add Electrolytes to Your Water: To maintain electrolyte balance, consider adding a pinch of high-quality sea salt to your water or using an electrolyte supplement. This is especially important during the first few weeks of the Carnivore Diet when your body is adjusting and may be losing more sodium and other electrolytes. You can also make a homemade electrolyte drink by combining water, a pinch of salt, and a squeeze of lemon.
3. Incorporate Bone Broth: Bone broth is an excellent source of electrolytes, particularly

sodium, and can be a soothing way to stay hydrated. Drinking a cup of bone broth daily can help replenish lost electrolytes while also providing collagen and other nutrients that support gut and joint health.

4. Monitor Your Urine Color: Keep an eye on the color of your urine as a simple way to gauge your hydration status. Aim for light yellow to clear urine, which indicates that you're adequately hydrated. If your urine is consistently dark, increase your water intake and consider adding electrolytes.

5. Eat Hydrating Foods: While the Carnivore Diet focuses on animal products, certain foods within this category can contribute to your hydration. For example, fish and seafood have a higher water content compared to red meats. Additionally, incorporating gelatinous cuts of meat and bone broth can help support hydration.

6. Adjust Hydration Based on Activity Level: If you're physically active, particularly in hot or humid environments, you'll need to increase your water and electrolyte intake to compensate for the fluids lost through sweat. Consider carrying a water bottle with added electrolytes during workouts and ensuring you rehydrate adequately afterward.

The Role of Hydration in Overall Health on the Carnivore Diet

Proper hydration is not just about avoiding dehydration; it plays a crucial role in optimizing your overall health on the Carnivore Diet. Adequate water and electrolyte intake support everything from digestion and nutrient absorption to cognitive function and physical performance.

Hydration also influences your body's ability to efficiently metabolize fats and proteins, which are central to the Carnivore Diet. Without sufficient water, the breakdown of these macronutrients can be impaired, potentially leading to digestive discomfort or reduced energy levels.

Moreover, staying well-hydrated helps your body manage the increased intake of protein on the Carnivore Diet by supporting kidney function and aiding in the excretion of waste products like urea. This is particularly important for preventing issues like kidney stones, which can occur if you're not drinking enough water to flush out these byproducts.

BEST PRACTICES FOR STAYING HYDRATED

Staying properly hydrated is one of the most crucial aspects of maintaining your health and well-being on the Carnivore Diet. Given the unique nature of this diet, which emphasizes high protein and fat intake with minimal carbohydrates, your hydration needs can differ significantly from those on a standard diet. Understanding how to effectively manage your water and electrolyte intake will help you avoid dehydration, support your overall health, and enhance your experience on the Carnivore Diet. Below, we'll explore the best practices for staying hydrated in a way that aligns with the dietary principles you're following.

1. Prioritize Consistent Water Intake

Water is essential for virtually every function in your body, from digestion and nutrient absorption to temperature regulation and waste elimination. On the Carnivore Diet, where carbohydrates are minimal and protein intake is high, your body's demand for water can increase. Protein metabolism, in particular, produces urea as a byproduct, which requires sufficient water for efficient excretion through the kidneys.

How to Stay Consistently Hydrated:
- **Start Your Day with Water:** Begin each day by drinking a glass of water to rehydrate after a night's sleep. This helps kickstart your metabolism and prepares your body for the day ahead.
- **Sip Water Throughout the Day:** Instead of waiting until you feel thirsty, aim to drink water consistently throughout the day. Always keep a water bottle with you as a reminder to stay hydrated.
- **Monitor Your Thirst:** While thirst isn't always the best indicator of hydration status, especially on a low-carb diet, it's still important to listen to your body's signals. If you're feeling thirsty, make sure to drink water right away.

2. Incorporate Electrolyte-Rich Beverages

As discussed earlier, electrolytes such as sodium, potassium, and magnesium play a crucial role in maintaining fluid balance and overall health. On the Carnivore Diet, where you might be losing more electrolytes due to the diuretic effect of a low-carb intake, it's important to replenish these essential minerals to prevent imbalances and support proper hydration.

How to Incorporate Electrolytes:
- **Add Salt to Your Water:** A simple and effective way to maintain sodium levels is to add a pinch of high-quality sea salt or Himalayan pink salt to your water. This can help balance fluids and prevent the common symptoms of low sodium, such as dizziness or headaches.
- **Make a Homemade Electrolyte Drink:** Combine water, a pinch of salt, and a squeeze of lemon juice to create a refreshing and hydrating beverage that replenishes electrolytes without added sugars or artificial ingredients.
- **Use Electrolyte Supplements:** Consider using an electrolyte powder or tablets that are free from sugars and artificial additives. These supplements are especially useful during periods of increased physical activity or hot weather, when you might lose more electrolytes through sweat.

3. Leverage Bone Broth for Hydration and Nutrients

Bone broth is a nutrient-dense, hydrating beverage that fits perfectly within the Carnivore Diet. It's rich in electrolytes like sodium and potassium, as well as collagen, amino acids, and other beneficial compounds that support joint health, gut integrity, and overall wellness.

How to Incorporate Bone Broth:
- **Enjoy Bone Broth Daily:** Aim to consume a cup of bone broth each day, either on its own or as a base for soups and stews. This can help maintain electrolyte balance while also providing additional nutrients that support your body's needs.
- **Use Bone Broth as a Hydration Tool:** If you're feeling dehydrated or notice symptoms like muscle cramps or headaches, try drinking bone broth to quickly restore electrolyte levels and improve hydration.

4. Balance Your Water and Electrolyte Intake

While it's important to drink plenty of water, it's equally important to balance this intake with adequate electrolytes. Drinking too much water without replenishing electrolytes can lead to a condition known as hyponatremia, where sodium levels in the blood become dangerously low.

How to Maintain Balance:
- **Avoid Overhydration:** Be mindful of drinking excessive amounts of water in a short period, especially without adding electrolytes. Focus on sipping water consistently throughout the day rather than consuming large quantities at once.
- **Pair Water with Electrolytes:** Whenever you're drinking water, especially after exercise or during hot weather, consider adding a pinch of salt or using an electrolyte supplement to maintain a healthy balance.

5. Adapt Hydration to Your Activity Level and Environment

Your hydration needs can vary significantly based on your activity level, climate, and individual physiology. Those who are more physically active or live in hot, humid environments will naturally require more water and electrolytes to stay hydrated.

How to Adjust Hydration Based on Activity:
- **Hydrate Before, During, and After Exercise:** Ensure that you're drinking water and replenishing electrolytes before starting physical activity, during your workout, and after you've finished. This helps prevent dehydration and supports optimal performance and recovery.
- **Consider Environmental Factors:** If you're in a hot or dry environment, increase your water and electrolyte intake to compensate for the additional fluid loss through sweating and evaporation.
- **Listen to Your Body:** Pay attention to signs of dehydration such as dry mouth, fatigue, and decreased urine output. Adjust your hydration strategy as needed to ensure you're meeting your body's demands.

6. Monitor Hydration Through Urine Color
One of the simplest and most effective ways to monitor your hydration status is by observing the color of your urine. This can give you a quick indication of whether you're drinking enough water or if you need to adjust your intake.

How to Use Urine Color as a Hydration Indicator:
- **Aim for Light Yellow:** Ideally, your urine should be light yellow to clear, which indicates proper hydration. Dark yellow or amber-colored urine suggests that you need to drink more water.
- **Be Mindful of Frequent Urination:** While staying hydrated is important, excessive urination might indicate that you're drinking too much water without adequate electrolytes. In such cases, consider increasing your electrolyte intake to help balance your hydration levels.

7. Make Hydration a Daily Habit
Consistency is key when it comes to staying hydrated on the Carnivore Diet. By making hydration a daily habit, you'll support your overall health, enhance your energy levels, and ensure that your body functions optimally.

How to Build a Hydration Habit:
- **Set Hydration Reminders:** Use alarms or apps to remind yourself to drink water regularly throughout the day. This can be especially helpful if you tend to get caught up in work or other activities and forget to hydrate.
- **Incorporate Hydration into Your Routine:** Tie hydration to existing habits, such as drinking a glass of water before each meal or upon waking up. This makes it easier to remember and maintain your hydration habits.
- **Track Your Intake:** Keep a log of your daily water and electrolyte intake to ensure you're meeting your hydration goals. This can also help you identify any patterns or adjustments needed based on your activity level and overall health.

CONCLUSION

Embarking on the Carnivore Diet is a transformative journey that goes beyond simply changing what you eat—it's about reshaping your relationship with food, health, and well-being. As we've explored throughout this guide, the Carnivore Diet offers a unique approach to nutrition that can lead to profound improvements in various aspects of your life, from increased energy levels and mental clarity to better digestion and overall health.

However, like any significant lifestyle change, it requires careful consideration, dedication, and a willingness to listen to your body's needs. The Carnivore Diet is not a one-size-fits-all solution, but rather a framework that you can tailor to your specific goals and circumstances. Whether you're seeking to manage a chronic condition, optimize your physical performance, or simply improve your quality of life, the principles of the Carnivore Diet provide a solid foundation upon which to build.

Throughout your journey, it's essential to remain mindful of the key factors that contribute to success on this diet. Proper hydration, balanced electrolyte intake, and attention to essential nutrients are all critical components that ensure your body functions at its best. By understanding the science behind the Carnivore Diet and applying the best practices we've discussed, you can navigate challenges with confidence and fully embrace the benefits that this way of eating has to offer.

As you move forward, remember that the Carnivore Diet is not just about following a strict set of rules—it's about developing a deeper understanding of what nourishes your body and how to achieve lasting health. Be patient with yourself, especially during the initial adjustment period, and be open to making adjustments as needed. Your journey on the Carnivore Diet is uniquely yours, and it's important to approach it with curiosity, flexibility, and a commitment to your well-being.

In conclusion, the Carnivore Diet has the potential to unlock a new level of vitality and health that you may have never experienced before. By focusing on nutrient-dense, animal-based foods, you're giving your body the tools it needs to thrive. Stay consistent, stay informed, and stay connected with your goals. With each step you take on this journey, you're not just changing your diet—you're transforming your life.

APPENDICES

GROCERY LISTS FOR EACH WEEK

Grocery Lists for Each Week for 90 Days
Embarking on a 90-day journey with the Carnivore Diet requires careful planning and preparation to ensure that you remain consistent and well-nourished throughout the process. A well-structured grocery list for each week will not only streamline your shopping but also help you focus on nutrient-dense foods, maintain variety, and keep your meals exciting and satisfying. Below, I'll guide you through detailed grocery lists for each week of your 90-day journey, with a focus on balancing simplicity, nutrient density, and the pleasure of eating.

Weeks 1-4: Building a Strong Foundation
The first month is all about laying the groundwork. You'll focus on the basics, ensuring you have a variety of meats, fats, and some organ meats to start with. This phase is designed to help your body adapt to the new way of eating.

Week 1: Basic Essentials
- **Beef:**
  1. Ground beef (80/20 blend) – 4 lbs
  2. Ribeye steaks – 3 steaks
  3. Beef liver – 1 lb
  4. Beef bones (for bone broth) – 2 lbs
- **Pork:**
  1. Pork chops – 4 chops
  2. Sugar-free bacon – 2 packs
- **Poultry:**
  1. Chicken thighs (bone-in, skin-on) – 3 lbs
  2. Whole chicken – 1 bird
- **Seafood:**
  1. Wild-caught salmon – 2 fillets
  2. Canned sardines – 4 cans
- **Eggs:**
  1. Large eggs – 2 dozen
- **Dairy:**
  2. Butter (grass-fed if possible) – 1 lb
  3. Heavy cream – 1 pint
- **Pantry Staples:**
  1. Sea salt
  2. Ghee or lard

Week 2: Expanding Variety
- **Beef:**
  1. Ground beef – 4 lbs
  2. New York strip steaks – 3 steaks
  3. Beef heart – 1 lb
  4. Oxtail – 2 lbs
- **Pork:**
  1. Pork shoulder – 4 lbs
  2. Pork belly – 2 lbs
- **Lamb:**
  1. Lamb chops – 2 lbs
  2. Lamb liver – 1 lb
- **Seafood:**
  1. Shrimp – 1 lb
  2. Cod fillets – 2 fillets
- **Eggs:**
  1. Large eggs – 2 dozen
- **Dairy:**
  1. Butter – 1 lb
  2. Hard cheese (optional) – 8 oz
- **Pantry Staples:**
  1. Sea salt
  2. Bone broth

Week 3: Introducing Higher Quality Meats
- **Beef:**
  1. Ground beef – 3 lbs
  2. Grass-fed ribeye steaks – 3 steaks
  3. Beef marrow bones – 2 lbs
  4. Beef tongue – 1-2 lbs
- **Pork:**
  1. Pork tenderloin – 2 lbs
  2. Sugar-free bacon – 2 packs
- **Poultry:**
  1. Duck breasts – 2 breasts
  2. Chicken wings – 3 lbs

- **Seafood:**
  1. Tuna steaks – 2 steaks
  2. Smoked salmon – 8 oz
- **Eggs:**
  1. Large eggs – 2 dozen
- **Dairy:**
  1. Butter – 1 lb
  2. Parmesan cheese (optional) – 8 oz
- **Pantry Staples:**
  1. Sea salt
  2. Ghee or lard

Week 4: Mastering Meal Prep
- **Beef:**
  1. Ground beef – 3 lbs
  2. Filet mignon – 3 steaks
  3. Beef liver – 1 lb
  4. Beef shank – 2 lbs

- **Pork:**
  1. Pork ribs – 2 racks
  2. Pork chops – 4 chops
- **Lamb:**
  1. Lamb shank – 2 lbs
  2. Lamb liver – 1 lb
- **Seafood:**
  1. Mussels or clams – 2 lbs
  2. Halibut fillets – 2 fillets
- **Eggs:**
  1. Large eggs – 2 dozen
- **Dairy:**
  1. Butter – 1 lb
  2. Goat cheese (optional) – 8 oz
- **Pantry Staples:**
  1. Sea salt
  2. Bone broth

Weeks 5-8: Refining Your Routine
As you move into the second month, your body is likely adjusting well to the Carnivore Diet. This period is ideal for refining your routine, experimenting with new cuts of meat, and ensuring that your meals are varied and nutrient-dense.

Week 5: Focus on Nutrient Density
- **Beef:**
  1. Ground beef – 4 lbs
  2. Grass-fed ribeye steaks – 3 steaks
  3. Beef kidney – 1 lb
  4. Beef ribs – 2 racks
- **Pork:**
  1. Pork belly – 3 lbs
  2. Pork sausage (sugar-free) – 2 packs
- **Poultry:**
  1. Whole duck – 1 bird
  2. Chicken thighs – 3 lbs
- **Seafood:**
  1. Wild-caught shrimp – 1 lb
  2. Salmon fillets – 2 fillets
- **Eggs:**
  1. Large eggs – 2 dozen
- **Dairy:**
  1. Butter – 1 lb
  2. Heavy cream – 1 pint
- **Pantry Staples:**
  1. Sea salt
  2. Lard or ghee

Week 6: Adding Organ Meats and Offal
- **Beef:**
  2. Ground beef – 4 lbs
  3. Sirloin steaks – 3 steaks
  4. Beef liver – 1 lb
  5. Beef heart or kidney – 1 lb
- **Pork:**
  1. Pork shoulder – 4 lbs
  2. Pork chops – 4 chops
- **Lamb:**
  1. Lamb liver – 1 lb
  2. Lamb chops – 2 lbs
- **Seafood:**
  1. Scallops – 1 lb
  2. Haddock fillets – 2 fillets
- **Eggs:**
  1. Large eggs – 2 dozen
- **Dairy:**
  1. Butter – 1 lb
  2. Hard cheese (optional) – 8 oz
- **Pantry Staples:**
  1. Sea salt
  2. Bone broth

Week 7: Emphasizing Quality and Variety
- **Beef:**
  1. Ground beef – 3 lbs
  2. Grass-fed filet mignon – 3 steaks
  3. Beef marrow bones – 2 lbs
  4. Beef shank – 2 lbs
- **Pork:**
  1. Pork belly – 3 lbs
  2. Sugar-free bacon – 2 packs
- **Poultry:**
  1. Turkey legs – 3 lbs
  2. Chicken wings – 3 lbs
- **Seafood:**
  1. Oysters – 1 dozen
  2. Cod fillets – 2 fillets
- **Eggs:**
  1. Large eggs – 2 dozen
- **Dairy:**
  1. Butter – 1 lb
  2. Heavy cream – 1 pint
- **Pantry Staples:**
  1. Sea salt
  2. Ghee or lard

Week 8: Advanced Nutrient Density
- **Beef:**
  1. Ground beef – 3 lbs
  2. New York strip steaks – 3 steaks
  3. Beef liver – 1 lb
  4. Beef tongue – 1-2 lbs
- **Pork:**
  1. Pork tenderloin – 3 lbs
  2. Pork ribs – 2 racks
- **Lamb:**
  1. Lamb chops – 2 lbs
  2. Lamb heart – 1 lb
- **Seafood:**
  2. Clams – 2 lbs
  3. Wild-caught salmon – 2 fillets
- **Eggs:**
  1. Large eggs – 2 dozen
- **Dairy:**
  1. Butter – 1 lb
  2. Goat cheese (optional) – 8 oz
- **Pantry Staples:**
  1. Sea salt
  2. Bone broth

Weeks 9-12: Mastery and Maintenance
In the final stretch of your 90-day Carnivore Diet, the focus should be on maintaining the progress you've made, fine-tuning your preferences, and ensuring that your meals continue to be satisfying and nutritious. This is also the time to solidify your long-term strategy for success.

Week 9: Continued Variety
- **Beef:**
  1. Ground beef – 4 lbs
  2. Ribeye steaks – 3 steaks
  3. Beef liver – 1 lb
  4. Beef short ribs – 2 racks
- **Pork:**
  1. Pork chops – 4 chops
  2. Sugar-free bacon – 2 packs
- **Poultry:**
  1. Chicken thighs – 3 lbs
  2. Whole chicken – 1 bird
- **Seafood:**
  1. Mussels – 2 lbs
  2. Scallops – 1 lb
- **Eggs:**
  1. Large eggs – 2 dozen
- **Dairy:**
  1. Butter – 1 lb
  2. Parmesan cheese (optional) – 8 oz
- **Pantry Staples:**
  1. Sea salt
  2. Ghee or lard

Week 10: Exploring New Cuts
- **Beef:**
  1. Ground beef – 4 lbs
  2. Sirloin steaks – 3 steaks
  3. Beef heart – 1 lb
  4. Beef ribs – 2 racks
- **Pork:**
  1. Pork shoulder – 4 lbs
  2. Pork belly – 3 lbs
- **Lamb:**
  1. Lamb liver – 1 lb
  2. Lamb shank – 2 lbs

- **Seafood:**
  1. Shrimp – 1 lb
  2. Cod fillets – 2 fillets
- **Eggs:**
  1. Large eggs – 2 dozen
- **Dairy:**
  1. Butter – 1 lb
  2. Heavy cream – 1 pint
- **Pantry Staples:**
  1. Sea salt
  2. Bone broth

Week 11: Mastering Meal Prep
- **Beef:**
  1. Ground beef – 3 lbs
  2. Grass-fed filet mignon – 3 steaks
  3. Beef tongue – 1-2 lbs
  4. Beef shank – 2 lbs
- **Pork:**
  1. Pork tenderloin – 3 lbs
  2. Sugar-free bacon – 2 packs
- **Poultry:**
  1. Duck breasts – 2 breasts
  2. Chicken wings – 3 lbs
- **Seafood:**
  1. Wild-caught tuna steaks – 2 steaks
  2. Halibut fillets – 2 fillets
- **Eggs:**
  1. Large eggs – 2 dozen

- **Dairy:**
  1. Butter – 1 lb
  2. Parmesan cheese (optional) – 8 oz
- **Pantry Staples:**
  1. Sea salt
  2. Ghee or lard

Week 12: Preparing for Long-Term Success
- **Beef:**
  1. Ground beef – 4 lbs
  2. Grass-fed ribeye steaks – 3 steaks
  3. Beef marrow bones – 2 lbs
  4. Beef liver – 1 lb
- **Pork:**
  1. Pork belly – 3 lbs
  2. Pork chops – 4 chops
- **Lamb:**
  1. Lamb chops – 2 lbs
  2. Lamb liver – 1 lb
- **Seafood:**
  1. Clams – 2 lbs
  2. Wild-caught salmon – 2 fillets
- **Eggs:**
  1. Large eggs – 2 dozen
- **Dairy:**
  1. Butter – 1 lb
  2. Goat cheese (optional) – 8 oz
- **Pantry Staples:**
  1. Sea salt
  2. Bone broth

Made in the USA
Las Vegas, NV
10 April 2025